Official as Teacher: An Investigation on the Newly Excavated Document of Legalist School in Qin China

以吏為師：
新出土法家教材新探

by Wen Ru Jia、Cheung Wai Po

溫如嘉、張偉保　著

總序

　　上世紀中葉，中國學術發展處於極其複雜的環境，新舊思想產生抗拒，卻又漸漸融和。學術研究方式惶惑於東西方模式，傳統與新式的路口中。一九四九年始，一群國內著名學者移遷香港，推展教育及學術，成就了北學南來的局面。錢穆先生的「新亞群組」就是其中一員，網羅頂尖兒的學者共同奮進，延續學術命脈。在錢穆先生等學者帶動及包融下，香港成為繼承中華文化及發展新儒學重要地方。

　　新亞書院及新亞研究所在港先後成立（1949及1953），研究所現址在土瓜灣農圃道是由國際著名的耶魯大學，及福特基金募捐所得。六十年代，新亞書院加入中文大學，成為了香港中文大學奠基的一員。一九七三年，成立新亞中學，同屬於新亞文化教育會之下的教育機構，目的是通過重組，以保持均衡而有聯繫性的中學至研究所教育的組織。

　　加入中大後，錢穆先生發覺中文大學的辦學理念與新亞書院創校的目的分歧甚大。遂於一九六三年，辭任中大新亞書院院長之職。一九八三年成立本院「新亞文商書院」，繼續以書院模式營運大學教育。在院教授老師，傳授知識道德，除耳提面命外，對同學的道德行為，心理發展，事業發展，承繼傳統文化等各方面均有所關顧。

　　本院出版《新亞文商學術叢刊》就是要保存不偏不倚的純學術研究刊物，舉凡有關中國文化、思想、經濟、歷史、文學、哲學、社會狀態發展與研究等，持平而具突破創新，有一定的學術水平者，本院因應院方財政狀況，資助及協助其著作出版。

　　二十一世紀，面對新的局面，資訊發達，對傳統學術研究帶來挑戰。

本院期望，能協助致力於學術研究，為中華文化出力，繼承新亞先賢的學術傳統，開拓未來發展道路的學者，建立園地，集中發表其學術成就，並方便學者透過此平臺，互相交流。所有出版書籍，均需要有學者專家推薦，院方才列入叢刊系列出版，以確保叢刊書籍的學術水平。

新亞文商書院院長

楊永漢

二〇二〇年冬

Abstract

In this thesis, under the historical-educational perspective, a group of teaching materials of Qin China was certainly taught. The content of the teaching materials was varied including legal documents, literacy, mathematics and ethical documents, and so on.

The basic tone of the education system of Qin China changed into learning Law as the propriety educational target. Legalist school played a key role in educational policies making, determining who to learn, what to learn, and how to learn. The guiding educational policies made by legalist's school were: "Burning the *Shi*《詩》and the *Shu*《書》to clarify the Law" and "Officials as teachers". The educational policy made a huge impact on the education system in ancient China.

Based on the newly excavated documentof Bamboo Slips of Qin Tomb of Shuihudi, the legal teaching material is a systematic group of legislative documents. It gathers numerous contents covering many aspects of society. They are both laws and legal teaching materials at the same time. All the legal teaching materials found in the newly excavated document of *the Eighteen Qin Statutes* 秦律十八篇 would be analyzed in this thesis part by part. Using the newly excavated document of *the Han Bamboo Slips of Zhang Jia Shan* 張家山漢墓竹簡 and *the chapter of Cang Jie of the Han bamboo slip of Beijing University* 北京大學藏漢簡, the literacy education of officials would be discussed. Mathematics education of Qin China would be divided into the problem of land and taxation, the problem of storage and goods, and the problem of labors and manufacturing industry for further discussion. At the same time, *the Way to Be a Good Official* 為吏之道 in Qin China, a guideof ethics for the officials, this newly excavated document has its characteristic of contents because it is not a legal document;.

The newly excavated document gives great help for us to understand the teaching materials of the legalist's school in Qin China. This thesis answers many academic questions base on the discovery of the newly excavated document.

TABLE OF CONTENTS

Chapter One

Introduction

1.1. The worthwhileness of the topic

This is a topic related to educational history, legal history, and intellectual history. As a student with a master's degree in Law, I tend to think about topics related to legal issues. During the period of my master's study, I noticed that many books and articles related to the newly excavated document of Qin and Han were published. And a good part of them was involved with the history of the Chinese traditional legal system. For my limited understanding at that time, I knew in every surviving hegemonic state the ruler succeeded, with the advice of the gentry-scholars, in stripping the aristocracy of their inherited privileges. And for Qin, with the advice of legalist-scholars, "law" was the main content for common people to learn during the Qin dynasty. The education system of Qin was so unique that I started to notice it was a fascinating issue. Gradually, those newly excavated documents of Qin attracted my attention. As time went by, I was honored to have the opportunity to further study in the faculty of education in UM, which brought me a new perspective to see those books and articles of newly excavated documents of Qin. In recent years, scholars in the field of bamboo-and-silk manuscripts have engaged in the study of book production, dissemination, and reception in early China. [1] Using these inaugural

---

[1] Marc Kalinowski, "Manuscript Culture in Present-day China and Its Significance to the Study of Chirographic Practices and Technical Literature in Late Warring States, Qin, and Han", Macau, Inaugural International Conference on New Philology and the study of Early China, 06/2016.

documents, some scholars studied them with the perspective of legality, philology, history, archaeology, or even sociology. However, there arefew studies with the perspectives of education history of teaching materials. Under this circumstance, and with the assistance of Prof. Cheung Wai-po, I had the chance to systematically review those materials of the newly excavated documents of Qin from the perspective of the education history of teaching materials.

1.2. Research Gaps

1.2.1. The historical period this article studies is about the one that before the Han dynasty, so-called Qin China. The reason for choosing that period is based on the development of the legalist school. In ancient China, deliberation and development on politics began to flourish in the sixth century B.C. Lots of schools flourished during the period of the Hundred Contending Schools 百家爭鳴 (551-221 B.C.), Legalist school was included. This epic period, overlapped with the Spring and Autumn periods 春秋時期 (772-476 B.C.) and the Warring States period 戰國時期 (475-221 B.C.), was the key moment for the blooming of the thoughts of the Chinese philosophers. Most of the major tenets of the Legalists were fully developed and formulated between 380 and 221 B.C., during the late Warring States period. Legalist school was developed and reached its peak on the unification of China by the Qin Empire. After the Qin Empire, the Han dynasty ruled, and then Legalist school was no longer in the dominant position of the society, starting to decline. So, the historical period of this article would be a set of Pre-Han according to the historical process of legalist school. Since we knew "Hundreds ousted, Confucianism dominating" was the feudal policy implemented by the emperor Wudi in Han 漢武帝, the research of Confucianism was blooming and countless. They covered different angles and aspects. And before Confucianism dominated, it was Legalist's School that had taken the dominant position in the Qin dynasty. The domination of Legalist's School was not very long and ceased abruptly, yet it still impacted China greatly with time passing. Even the studies of legalist were varied, few of them was researched under the perspective of education history of teaching materials.

1.2.2. China is a country with marvel history and its education system was well developed and advanced compared with other countries in ancient times. To study the ancient education history of China, we have to do systematic and in-depth research on teaching materials. There are the narrow meaning and the extensive meaning for teaching materials. The narrow meaning of teaching materials is the textbooks for the students, which are the core material for the curriculum. The extensive meaning for teaching materials is the materials that can extend knowledge and develop skills. Base on the antiquity, the teaching materials of Qin China was not formed as the narrow meaning of teaching materials with modern significance. Therefore, it is obvious for us to choose the extensive meaning of teaching materials in this research.

1.2.3. Bamboo and wood were the earliest materials used for books and documents in China and had a strong and far-reaching impact on

Chinese culture.[2] In recent decades, a huge number of newly excavated documents were discovered, including bamboo, silk, wooden, and so on. Lots of historical relics were excavated and most of them are related to early Chinese culture. Once some documents were found in the ancient tomb, our understanding of ancient China was deepened or even changed. They largely supplement the materials handed down from ancient times. The academic area in this filed at present can be called the time of *Double evidence method* 雙重證據法, using the new materials underground "地下之新材料" to supply the material on paper "紙上之材料".[3] Up to now, there are several newly excavated document of Qin, including *Qin bamboo slips of Yunmeng Shuihudi* 雲夢睡虎地秦簡, *Qin bamboo slips of Longgang* 龍崗秦簡, *Qin wooden tablets of Qingchuanhaojiaping* 青川郝家坪秦牘, *Qin bamboo slips of Liye* 里耶秦簡 and *Qin bamboo slips of Yuelu* 嶽麓秦簡, *Qin bamboo slips of Beijing University* 北大藏秦簡. All these can enrich the materials handed down from ancient times.

In the meanwhile, they play key roles to restore the historical facts. The contents of the newly excavated documents of Qin are varied, for some have more content of legal historical data and some have less or scattered. More than half of the content is directly or indirectly related to the legal system. Legalist's content of governance probably constitutes the earliest theory of totalitarianism. "The Legalists

---

2   *Tsuen-Hsuin Tsien* 錢存訓, *Written on Bamboo & Silk, The Beginnings of Chinese Books and Inscriptions, Second Edition, Chicago, University of Chicago Press, 2004, p.96.*

3   Wang Guowei 王國維, *Gu Shi Xin Zheng*《古史新證》, Changsha, Hu Nan Renmin Press, 2010, p.2.

conceived of law primarily as a penal tool the ruler uses to maintain his governance over his subjects and propounded the rule by law, not the rule of law."[4] That made "law" unique teaching materials in Qin. When Qin was expanding rapidly, it needed more and more officials to govern the land and maintain the social order. During the Qin period, regardless of the transformation of the official system, as an official with a specific function or anyone of humble origins wanted to be an official, so the duration of learning was unavoidable. No matter which way he chose to learn, an official should be qualified and should be able to deal with certain issues. So, the teaching materials we talk about in this research are mainly surrounded by the teaching materials for officials. In the meanwhile, the education policies of Qin were "law as education" 以法為教 and "officials as teachers" 以吏為師, meaning law was learned by the common people under the influence of legalist's school. The understanding of the newly excavated documents as teaching materials could better help us to resort to the original condition of the education history of Qin.

1.2.4. The impact of the Legalist school is enormous, even after thousands of years till now. There are lots of books and articles focusing on the newly excavated documents of Pre-Han, and the academic areas includethe legality, philology, history, archaeology, or even sociology. Some scholars use the newly excavated documents to analyze the

---

4 Zhengyuan Fu, *China's Legalists the Earliest Totalitarians and Their Art of Ruling*, New York, M.E. Sharpe, 1996, p.12.

education system of Pre-Han under the perspective of intellectual history; however, not too many analyze the education system of Qin under the perspective of teaching materials. The Legalists implemented the total subordination among the plebian for the ruler and facilitated the domination of the state over society, which led the rulers to take Legalists' ideas and made the policies of *law as education* and *officials as teachers*. The common people learned from no one but the officials and for nothing but the law. If people wanted to be officials, they must meet certain educational levels. So, what officials of Qin should learn, how they learn, how they teach the people, and what they teach to the people become questions for us to figure out. And as far as the writer was concerned, using the newly excavated documents of Qin and the materials handed down from ancient times to try to better resort to the original condition of teaching materials of Qin could deepen the understanding of the education system of that period, which can deepen the understanding of the history of education and broaden the impact of the history of teaching materials.

1.3. Literature Review

The exiting newly excavated documents of Pre-Han are numbered. A variety of studies of these newly excavated documents of Pre-Han are published. All the related studies are helpful to our research; we can generally categorize them in the following ideas:

1.3.1. The most common type of the studies of newly excavated documents of Qin is the textual research and explanation. The most significant finding of excavated documents of Qin since the 1970s was the discovery in Shuihudi, Yunmeng, Hubei in 1974. The finding from Shuihudi of 1100 bamboo tablets, containing mostly legal and historical materials, dated to 306-217 B.C., is considered rather important, as these documents are the laws and statutes of the Qin dynasty, which were not known before.[5] There are lots of textual research and explanation of Qin bamboo slips of Shuihudi. Such as: *Remnants of Ch'in Law: An Annotated Translation of the Ch'in Legal and Administrative Rules of the 3rd Century B.C. Discovered in Yun-meng Prefecture*[6], *The study of the intellectual history of Chu Bamboo and Qin Bamboo during Warring States*《戰國楚簡與秦簡之思想史研究》[7], *Research of Qin Bamboo Slip of Yunmeng*《雲夢秦簡研究》[8], *The Compilation and Research of the Qin Bamboo Slips of Academy of Yuelu*《岳麓書院藏秦簡的整理與研究》[9], *The Organization and Research of the Widely Scattered Qin Bamboo Slips during Warring States*《散見戰國秦漢簡帛法律文獻整理與研

5　Tsuen-Hsuin Tsien 錢存訓, *Written on Bamboo & Silk, The Beginnings of Chinese Books and Inscriptions, Second Edition*, Chicago, University of Chicago Press, 2004, p.103.

6　A.F.P. Huleswe, *Remnants of Ch'in Law: An Annotated Translation of the Ch'in Legal and Administrative Rules of the 3rd Century B.C. Discovered in Yun-meng Prefecture*, Hu-pei Province, in 1975, Leiden, E. J. Brill Publisher, 1985.

7　KunihiroYuasa 湯淺邦弘, *The study of the intellectual history of Chu Bamboo and Qin Bamboo during Warring States*《戰國楚簡與秦簡之思想史研究》, Taipei, Wan Juan Lou, 2006.

8　The editing department of Zhonghua Book Company中華書局編輯部, *Research of Qin Bamboo Slip of Yunmeng*《雲夢秦簡研究》, Beijing, Zhonghua Book Company, 1981.

9　Chen Songchang etc. 陳松長等, *The Compilation and Research of the Qin Bamboo Slips of Academy of Yuelu*《嶽麓書院藏秦簡的整理與研究》, Shanghai, Zhongxi Press, 2014.

究》[10], *The study of thoughts and systems of Qin Bamboo Slip of Yunmeng*《雲夢秦簡中思想與制度鈎摭》[11], *Bamboo Slips of No.247 Tomb of Zhangjiashan*《張家山漢墓竹簡[二四七號墓]》[12], *The Copy of the Legality of Ancient China*《中國古代法制叢抄》[13], *The Proofread and Citation of the Qin Bamboo Slips of Liye*《里耶秦簡牘校釋》[14], *The First Exploration of Chu Bamboo Slips of Baoshan*《包山楚簡初探》[15], *The Correction of Exegesis of the Qin Bamboo Slips of Liye*《里耶秦簡校詁》[16], *The Proofread of Chu Bamboo Slips of Guodian*《郭店楚簡校讀記》[17], *The Macro and Micro of Qin's Confucianism of Chu Bamboo Slips of Guodian*《郭店楚簡先秦儒學宏微觀》.[18] Also, there have been studies explaining

---

10 Li Mingxiao 李明曉 and Zhao jiuxiang 趙久湘,*The Organization and Research of the Widely Scattered Qin Bamboo Slips during Warring States*《散見戰國秦漢簡帛法律文獻整理與研究》, Chongqing, Southwest China Normal University Press, 2011.

11 Yu Zongfa 余宗發, *The study of thoughts and systems of Qin Bamboo Slip of Yunmeng*《雲夢秦簡中思想與制度鈎摭》, Taipei, Wenjin Press, 1992.

12 The Organization team of No.247 Tomb of Zhangjiashan 張家山二四七號漢墓之整理小組,*Bamboo Slips of No.247 Tomb of Zhangjiashan*《張家山漢墓竹簡[二四七號墓]》, Beijing,Cultural Relics Press, 2006.

13 Pu Jian 蒲堅,*The Copy of the Legality of Ancient China*《中國古代法制叢抄》, Beijing, Guangming Daily Press, 2001.

14 Chen Wei 陳偉, *The Proofread and Citation of the Qin Bamboo Slips of Liye*《里耶秦簡牘校釋》, Wuhan, Wuhan University Press, 2012.

15 Chen Wei 陳偉, *The First Exploration of Chu Bamboo Slips of Baoshan*《包山楚簡初探》, Wuhan, Wuhan University Press, 1996.

16 Wang Huanlin 王煥林, *The Correction of Exegesis ofthe Qin Bamboo Slips of Liye*《里耶秦簡校詁》, Beijing, China Federation of Literary and Art Circles Press, 2007.

17 Li Ling 李零, *The Proofread of Chu Bamboo Slips of Guodian*《郭店楚簡校讀記》, Beijing, China Renmin University Press, 2007.

18 Gu Shikao 顧史考, *The Macro and Micro of Qin's Confucianism of Chu Bamboo Slips of Guodian*《郭店楚簡先秦儒學宏微觀》, Shanghai, Shanghai Guji Press, 2012.

the newly excavated documents. One example is that scholar Gao Min 高敏 distinguishes the differences between Qin Law of Shang Yang and Qin Law of Qin bamboo slips of Yunmeng in his book titled *the First Exploration of Qin bamboo Slips of Yunmeng*《雲夢秦簡初探》.[19] As an important part of the materials handed down from ancient times of Legalist school, Qin Law of Shang Yang is directly related to the law as education of Qin and it was a major teaching material for the people of Qin. He pointed out that there were three differences: 1. some articles of Qin Law of Shang Yang could not be found in the Qin bamboo slips of Yunmeng; 2. the classification of these two were different; 3.He confirmed that some content of the Qin bamboo slips of Yunmeng was not composed by the Qin Law of Shang Yang. It better resorts to the understanding of the core work of Legalist School and clears the accuracy of the content of Qin Law using newly excavated documents of Qin. As we know that the education policy of Qin was "law as education" 以法為教 and "officials as teachers"[2021]以吏為師, knowing the textual research and explanations of Qin helps us to understand the exact contents of the teaching materials of Qin.

19 Gao Min 高敏, *The First Exploration of Qin bamboo Slips*《雲夢秦簡初探》, Zhengzhou, Henan Renmin Press, 1979.

20 〔Han〕Sima Qian〔漢〕司馬遷, *Shi Ji/Records of the History*《史記》, Xuchang, Zhongzhou Guji Press, 1996, pp. 714-721. (*No.27 of Collected Biographies of Li Si* 《李斯列傳第二十七》)

21 Takigawa Kametaro 瀧川資言, *Shiki Kaichu Kosho*《史記會注考證》, Beijing, New World Press, 2009, p.3939.

1.3.2. The philology of Pre-Han is a deeply researched topic. China is a country of characters, a country of recording, so it could be called a country of literature.[22] In the book of *Chinese writing*《文字學概要》, written by scholar Qiu Xigui 裘錫圭, some philological issues related to Qin were mentioned. Stone inscriptions, bronze inscriptions, seals and sealing-clay inscriptions, pottery inscriptions, lacquer-ware inscriptions, bamboo slip, wooden tablets, and silk manuscript texts were discussed as Chinese characters.[23] People of Han had to literate 9000 characters to become an official (能諷書九千字以上，乃得為吏),[24] those materials that officials needed to learn were teaching materials. From the handed-down materials of ancient China, Lord Li Si wrote *Cang Jie Pian*《倉頡篇》, we consider it to be the learning material for characters. Some scholars[25][26][27] did researches on the philology of Qin, and they find out that a qualified Qin official should learn some certain characters. These research outcomes give us a glimpse of the teaching material of

---

22 稻畑耕一郎, "The handed down and excavated documents of Chinese ancient areas" 《中國古代領域中的傳世典籍與出土資料》, Macau, Inaugural International Conference on New Philology and the study of Early China, 06/2016.

23 Qui Xigui 裘錫圭, *Chinese Writing*《文字學概要》, New Haven, Bird track Press, 2000.

24 〔Han〕Ban Gu〔漢〕班固, *Han Shu/History of the Former Han*《漢書》, Zhengzhou, Zhongzhou Guji Press, 2007, p.598.

25 Boltz, William G. *The Origin an Early Development of the Chinese Writing System*, American Oriental Series, vol. 78, New Haven, Conn., American Oriental Society, 1994.

26 MartinKern, *The Stele Inscriptions of Ch'in Shih-huang: Text and Ritual in Early Chinese Imperial Representation*, New Haven, CT, American Oriental Society, 2000.

27 Lewis, Mark Edward. *Writing and Authority in Early China*, Albany, State University of New York Press, 1999.

the literacy of Pre-Qin China. The books of *Ji Jiu*《急就篇》[28], *History of Education of Language and Literature of ancient China* 《中國古代語文教育史》[29], *A General Survey of Qin Characters* 《秦文字通論》[30], *Ten Topics of Unearthed Ancient Documents of China*《中國出土古文獻十講》[31], *New Sources of Early Chinese History: An Introduction to the Reading of Inscriptions and Manuscripts*[32], *Unearthed Documents and Literature of Qin*《出土文獻與秦國文學》[33] are all related to the philology of Qin.

1.3.3. In some studies of the history of mathematics in China, we can find that mathematics is a curriculum in ancient China.[34][35][36] Also, mathematics was a curriculum for the official of Qin. In Qin, the

---

28 Shi You史遊,*Ji Jiu*《急就篇》, Chang Sha, Yuelu College Press, 1989.

29 Zhang Longhua張隆華, Zeng Zhongshan曾仲珊, *History of Education of Language and Literature of ancient China*《中國古代語文教育史》, Chengdu, Sichuan Education PressSichuan Education Press, 2003.

30 Wang Hui王輝, Chen Shaorong 陳紹榮, Wang Wei 王偉, *A General Survey of Qin Characters* 《秦文字通論》, Beijing, Zhonghua Book Company, 2016.

31 Qiu Xigui 裘錫圭, *Ten Topics of Unearthed Ancient Documents of China*《中國出土古文獻十講》, Shanghai, Fudan University Press, 2004.

32 Edward L. Shaughnessy, *New Sources of Early Chinese History: An Introduction to the Reading of Inscriptions and Manuscripts*《中國古文字學導論》, Berkeley, Institute of East Asian Studies and Society for the Study of Early China, 1997.

33 Ni Jinbo倪晉波, *Unearthed Documents and Literature of Qin*《出土文獻與秦國文學》, Beijing, Cultural Relics Press, 2015.

34 Guo Shuchun 郭書春, *Translation and Annotation of Jiuzhang Suanshu or the Nine Chatpters on Mathematical Procedures,*《九章算術譯註》, Shanghai, Shanghai Guji Press, 2009.

35 Wang Yusheng 王渝生, *History of Chinese Mathematics*《中國算學史》, Shanghai, Shanghai Renmin Press, 2006.

36 Zou Dahai鄒大海, *The Rising of Chinese Mathematics and the Mathematics of Pre-Qin*, Zhengzhou, Hebei science technology Press, 2001.

government had a group of officers in charge of accounting. We call these officers Ji 計, Kuai 會, Jishu 計數, Kuaiji 會計, Zhiji 職計, Suanfa 演算法. We can find solid evidence according to the Qin bamboo slips collected by Peking University 北京大學 and the Qin bamboo slips collected by Yuelu College 嶽麓書院. Some conversational issues of mathematics of Chinese history were sorted out by the newly excavated documents of Qin. The formula of the corresponding problem, such as Yuelu College's bamboo slips of No. 0458 (十六兩一斤。三十斤一鈞。四鈞一石。) is the matrix of weight;[37] taxation problem, such as bamboo slips of No. 0537 (取程，八步一斗。今乾之九升。述（術）曰：十田八步者，以為實。以九升為法。如法一步。不盈步，以法命之。) is the way to calculate cultivated land, and other kinds of mathematics problems are analyzed.[38] With these research studies of mathematics of Qin, it would be helpful for us to try to resort to the original teaching material within the education system in Pre-Han.

1.3.4. Law School Study of Qin 秦律令學 is a well-studied topic; these studies are valuable for this topic. Since Qin followed the rule of "Law as education", learning the law of Qin is at a certain level learning the teaching materials of Qin. The newly excavated documents provide us with the precise materials. From the

---

37 Chen Songchang etc. 陳松長等, *The Compilation and Research of the Qin Bamboo Slips of Academy of Yuelu*《嶽麓書院藏秦簡的整理與研究》, Shanghai, Zhongxi Press, 2014, p.28. The content of bamboo slips of No. 0458/0303/0646.

38 Xiao Can 蕭燦, *The research of Mathematics of Qin bamboo slips collected by Yuelu College*, Beijing, Social Sciences Academic Press (China), 2015.

perspective of the completeness and quantity of the legal documents of Qin, *Qin bamboo slips of Yunmeng Shuihudi* are very impressive. *The Eighteen Qin Statutes* 秦律十八篇, *the statutes concerning Checking* 效律, *Miscellaneous Excerpts from Qin Statutes* 秦律雜抄, *Answers to Questions Concerning Qin Statutes* 法律答問 and *Models for Sealing and Investigating* 封診式 of Qin Law caused more concerns from the scholars of Law school study of Qin. Different versions of translation of *Qin Law of Qin bamboo slips of Yunmeng Shuihudi*, such as *the Remnants of Ch'in Law*,[39] were published. Other than translation, the analysis, and research of Law School Study of Qin were published as well. Scholars tried different ways to analyze the law school study of Qin. Some scientifically organized the original excavated documents into the way that other people without the background of paleography could read.[40] Some combined Qin Law and Legalist's School to do the research, trying to systematically describe the general theoretical principle of legalist through Qin Law and the legal practice of Qin.[41] Some separated the Qin Law into different topics for further discussion of the Law school study of Qin, trying to find out the relationship among Qin Law, its

---

39 A.F.P. Huleswe, *Remnants of Ch'in Law: An Annotated Translation of the Ch'in Legal and Administrative Rules of the 3rd Century B.C. Discovered in Yun-meng Prefecture*, Hu-pei Province, in 1975, Leiden, E. J. Brill Publisher, 1985.

40 The organization team of bamboo slips of Qin tomb of Shuihudi 睡虎地秦墓竹簡整理小組, *Bamboo slips of Qin tomb of Shuihudi*《睡虎地秦墓竹簡》, Beijing, Cultural Relics Press, 1978.

41 Li Jin 栗勁, *The General Theory of Qin Law*《秦律通論》, Jinan, Shangdong Renmin publisher, 1985.

society, and the punishment of Qin Law.[42] As the thesis mentioned above, Qin Law would be important for our study of teaching material of Qin, so, the research of Law School Study of Qin would be valuable.

In the meanwhile, except Law School Study of Qin, Law School Study of Han could be lessons to learn. In the Han dynasty, the chancellor Xiao He makes Han Law based on Qin Law. Even the Han Law failed to be handed down from past generations, and in 1983, more than 500 pieces of bamboo slips were found in the Han tomb of Zhangjiashan, Hubei 湖北張家山漢墓. These Han bamboo slips were titled as *the Two Year Laws*《二年律令》. The explanation of Two-Year Law was studied.[43] The relationship between Qin Law and Han Law was studied.[44]

1.4. Research Question

The teaching materials of Legalist in Qin China are important to the history of education. Fromthe document analytic angle, I combed the fundamental sequence of ideas that Legalist's School teaching material developed. There are two levels the research would analyze. This thesis is

---

[42] Cao Lvning曹旅寧, *New discovery of Qin Law*《秦律新探》, Beijing, China Social Sciences Press, 2002.

[43] Zhu Honglin 朱紅林, *The Explanation Collection on the Two Year Laws of Zhangjiashan Bamboo Slips*《張家山漢簡〈二年律令〉》集釋, Beijing, Social Sciences Academic Press (China), 2005.

[44] Wang Yanhui 王彥輝,*The Research of Han society and the Two Year Laws of Zhangjiashan*《張家山漢簡〈二年律令〉與漢代社會研究》, Beijing, Zhonghua Book Company, 2010. pp.1-4.

trying to answer the following questions:

a. What were the teaching materials of Legalist's School for the rulers in Qin China?

The upper class: ruler's teaching materials. The legalist ideal social order is also like an animal farm where the ruler is the only owner.[45]The ruler learned those books which could make them better rule the country. We could find the necessary content from the handed-down materials.

b. What were the teaching materials of Legalist's School for the officials in Qin China?

The teaching materials of the Legalist's School for the official in Qin China were not clear writings. However, we can try to build it up by combining the handed down material and the newly excavated documents. There were different subjects of the teaching materials, including 1. the discovery of *Qin bamboo slips of Yunmeng Shuihudi,* which could be excellent proof for us to find out the answer to this question. We can at least tell that there are ten kinds of documents of *Qin bamboo slips of Yunmeng Shuihudi,* except *the Annals of mind* 編 年紀, and all other nine kinds are related to the legal teaching materials of Legalist's School for the official in Qin China. 2. the teaching materials of literacy of Legalist's School; 3. the teaching materials of mathematics of Legalist's School; 4. The teaching materials of officials' morality of Legalist's School. The writer will

---

45 Zhengyuan Fu, *China's Legalists the Earliest Totalitarians and Their Art of Ruling*, New York, M.E. Sharpe, 1996, p.107.

take a cautious look at them and try to answer this question.

c. What were the teaching materials of Legalist's School for the people in Qin China?

To guarantee the totalitarian domination on the plebian of the ruler, the Legalist built up the policy system to ensure the state's power could be put into force and as extending over all aspects of social life. Through such power, all the individual subjects among the state would be controlled and manipulated by the ruler. Thus, within the Legalist's prescribed totalitarian society, the lives of the subjects are ideally under the total scrutiny and control of the state. Teaching the people nothing but only limited knowledge might be a good way to maintain the ruler's totalitarian. So, the teaching material of the people was limited to "Law as education".

1.5. Methodology

The documentary method would be the most important method used in this thesis. Both newly excavated documents and handed-down materials from ancient times would be systematically and scientifically used to find out the whole picture of the teaching materials under the influence of Legalist's School of Qin. Surrounding the main methods, we are going to talk about the development of Legalist's School, trying to understand the influence of the Legalist's School for Qin's education. This research is trying to find out the teaching materials of the officials using the materials that we study now. In the meanwhile, double evidence method would be used as well. The writer would combine newly excavated documents of Qin and handed- down materiasl from ancient China, and take other archaeological discoveries of

Qin as a reference, to find out the original situation of teaching material of Qin under the perspective of education history. Besides, a comparative study method would be used in this research. The author would compare the teaching materials of legal document between Pre-Han and present time , and with a great amount of newly excavated documents being found in different locations, the author would compare the similar content of those teaching materials among different newly excavated documents, trying to find out if geographic position influences the structure of teaching materials.

Chapter Two
The legalist school in Pre-Qin and Qin

Traditionally speaking, Chinese historians have claimed that some hundred schools of philosophy contended during this era 百家爭鳴. But talking about China's intellectual development, most Chinese scholars would also agree that, in political philosophy, only 4 major schools exerted a significant influence: the Confucian 儒家, the Moist 墨家, the Daoist 道家, and the Legalist 法家. The Legalist school played a major role in the education system during the pre-Qin and Qin dynasty period.

Most of the major tenets of the Legalists were fully developed and formulated between 380 and 230 B.C., during the late Warring States period. If we discuss the legalists' political philosophy, both the supremacy of authority and the centralization of power in the sovereignty would be the main themes. According to *History of the Former Han*, Legalist school remains 217 chapters.[1] They implemented the total subordination among the plebian for the ruler and helped with the domination of the state over society. The Legalist tenets of governance probably constitute the earliest theory of totalitarianism, and their ideas exerted an influential impact on the institutional and systematical policy-developing building of the Chinese bureaucratic empire. And on Chinese political practice throughout the imperial era, their ideas also had an important say. The legalists conceived of law primarily as a penal tool the ruler uses to maintain his governance over

---

1   〔Han〕Ban Gu〔漢〕班固, *Han Shu/History of the Former Han*《漢書》, Shanghai, Shanghai Guji Press, 12/2003, p.1197.

his subjects and propounded the rule by law, not the rule of law.[2] The works of the Legalists school are mainly about the maintenance and consolidation of the power of the ruler. There were several famous and eminent Legalists known during pre-Qin China, and the writings of them comprised a set of consistent themes and doctrines of Legalists' school. The famous and eminent Legalists were inclusive of Guan Zhong 管仲, Li Kui 李悝, Wu Qi 吳起, Shen Dao 慎到, Shen Buhai 申不害, Shang Yang 商鞅, Li Si 李斯, and Han Fei 韓非. Ban Gu 班固 listed 10 Legalists, including Li Kui, Shang Yang, Shen Buhai, Shen Dao, Han Fei, and others.[3] The pre-Qin Legalists were incumbents of prominently positioned political offices; many of them were chancellors (such as Shang Yang) and chief ministers. They fulfilled the needs of the rules admirably by making political reform from the bottom level of the society to the aristocracy when China was set in a war of all against all among the various states. The Legalist school gave a great impact on education, policymaking, and social formation. It was a key to those states for survival and striving for supremacy among other states.

2.1. Li Kui 李悝

Li Kui was the chancellor of Wei state during that time. It was ruled by Wei Wen Hou 魏文侯.

2　Zhengyuan Fu, *China's Legalists the Earliest Totalitarians and Their Art of Ruling*, New York, M.E. Sharpe, 1996.

3　〔Han〕Ban Gu〔漢〕班固, *Han Shu/History of the Former Han*《漢書》, Shanghai, Shanghai Guji Press, 12/2003, p.1197.

2.1.1.   The biography of Li Kui

Li Kui helped Wei state to carry out   the political reform targeting the aristocracy. His reform made a great success: 1. Stripping of the privileges of hereditary from the aristocracy; 2. Electing those with the capability to govern the society; 3. Rewarding people with contribution; 4. Encouraging people to develop agriculture and providing them with knowledge about agriculture 盡地力之教; 5. Paying for grain in harvest year from farmers and sold the grain at low prices in lean year 收有餘以補不足; etc.[4]

In the book of *the Han Shu*, Ban Gu put *Li Zi*《李子》 on the first position of the Legalist school. There were 32 chapters of *Li Zi* which were written by Li Kui; however, the doctrine of Li Kui was lost and we could not track the origin.   Ba Gu said that Li Kui was the chancellor of Wei Wen Hou, and he made the economy of Wei state affluent   and helped to strengthen the military power of Wei state.[5] Other than these, he made a huge impact on Legalist school for the first written law code of squirearchy in Chinese history.

2.1.2.   The doctrine of Li Kui

We considered that Li Kui was supposed to be the starter of legalist school, based on the fact that he was the first one who edited a comparatively complete statute book. [6] As an outstanding figure of Legalist school at the

---

4   〔Han〕Ban Gu〔漢〕班固, *Han Shu/History of the Former Han*《漢書》, Shanghai, Shanghai Guji Press, 12/2003, pp.790-791.

5   〔Han〕Ban Gu〔漢〕班固, *Han Shu/History of the Former Han*《漢書》, Shanghai, Shanghai Guji Press, 12/2003, p.1197.

6   Wang Hongbin王宏斌, *Emperor's Art· Han Fei Zi and Chinese Culture*《中國帝王術·〈韓非子〉與中國文化》, Kaifeng, Henan University Press, 1995, p.6.

beginning of Warring State, Li Kui categorized all the legal status of every state, named *Fa Jing*《法經》. [7] There were six parts of *Fa Jing* including *Law ofrob*《盜法》, *Law of thief* 《賊法》, *Law of imprisoning*《囚法》, *Law of arrest*《捕法》, *Law of Za*《雜法》 and *Law of Ju* 《具法》. The first four parts were the main content of the book, and they systematically listed how to lock up and track down robbers and thieves, and it was a book using legal measures to protect the benefits of the squirearchy. Some particular statutes were made to prevent or punish the aristocracy for damaging the benefits of landlords. Take the regulation in *the Law of Za,* for example. , It pointed out that, borrowing money but did not return 假借不廉 was a crime; gambling 博戲 was forbidden, using luxury life utensil which arrogated the hierarchy 淫奢踰制 should be punished, etc.[8] These statutes were mainly aimed to limit the aristocracy.

We know that the work of Shang Yang 商鞅 in his early stage was very similar to the thought of Li Kui. Shang Yang changed the name of the status from the *Fa* of Li Kui to the *Lv* of Shang Yang 改法為律. We can find related information from the handed-down documents of *the Criminal Law of the History of Jin*《晉書·刑法志》 and *the Exposition of Tang Penal Code*《唐律疏議·名例一》. Both of the articles are talking about the change from *Fa* to *Lv*. Despite the name change, the content was almost the same containing 6 kinds of regulations, including *Dao*《盜》, *Zei* 《賊》, *Qiu*

---

7   Institute for Chinese Ancient Legal Document of China University of Political Science and Law 中國政法大學法律古籍整理研究所, *Translation and Annotation of Criminal Laws in Generations of China*《中國歷代刑法志註譯》, Changchun, Jilin Renmin Press, p.74.

8   Institute for Chinese Ancient Legal Document of China University of Political Science and Law 中國政法大學法律古籍整理研究所, *Translation and Annotation of Criminal Laws in Generations of China*《中國歷代刑法志註譯》, Changchun, Jilin Renmin Press, pp.49-134.

《囚》, *Bu*《捕》, *Za*《雜》, *and Ju* 《具》.

In the handed-down documents, the 6 kinds of regulations of *Fa Jing* were changed into a book of Xiao He 蕭何 named *Jiu Zhang Lv*《九章律》 with 9 chapters. Except for the 6 kinds of regulations, 3 chapters were added , including *Hu*《戶律》with law of registered residence, taxes and marriage; *Xing*《興律》with law of conscription of corvee, urban defense and guarding; *Jiu*《廄律》with law of rear livestock and postal delivering system.

Although the doctrine of Li Kui was lost we could still tell that he made a difference in the development of legalist school. Firstly, *Fa Jing* was an outstanding achievement during the political change in the early period of warring states.   It was a comprehensive representation of the legal structure during that period. In the meanwhile, as an important content of the political reform, *Fa Jing* went with the tide of historical development and it was the legal basis consultation for the feudal dynasties to come. And lastly, the style, system, and content of *Fa Jing* became a basic foundation for the later compilation of Law code.

2.2. Shang Yang 商鞅

Shang Yang was both a prominent statement in the Warring state period and a famous representative of the Legalists school.

2.2.1. The biography of Shang Yang

Shang Yang (? – 338 B.C.) was born in a royal family in the Wei state 衛國, so he was called Wei Yang 衛鞅, meaning the Yang from the Wei state. In the meanwhile, according to the tradition, he was also called Gong Sun Yang 公孫鞅, based on the family name Gong Sun 公孫. Subsequently, he was given a fiefdom of Shang due to his battle feats of Battle of Hexi 河西之戰. And then he was called Shang Yang, which means Yang was the lord of Shang. Aamong the minority of the legalists, he was able to ascend to a political position and sufficiently displayed his ability in history of pre-Qin.[9] He was born in a chaotic period, and his life experience, which from the aristocracy of noble level fell low to be a retainer of the governor, and his country from a weak state got into a strong state, made a huge influence on his thought formation and political view.[10]

When Shang Yang was young, he learned the practical learning, including "Xing Ming Zhi Xue"/Learning of the Form and Name 刑名之學, "Za Jia"/Eclecticism 雜家, "Bing Jia"/the School of War 兵家, etc. During the period when he was a junior officer in the Wei state, Shang Yang studied the reforms of Li Kui 李悝 and Wu Qi 吳起, who were both famous and eminent Legalists, and absorbed these practical learning into his thought in the further time. Duke Xiao of state Qin 秦孝公 issued decrees calling for persons of wisdom to help him to reform and enhance the state power. Shang Yang was attracted and moved to Qin state, and eventually, Duke Xiao of state Qin appreciated the intelligence of Shang Yang and appointed him to launch the reform of Qin. With the full support of the duke, Shang Yang was able to implement a series of reforms that resulted in fundamental changes in the social and political institutions of the Qin state. Like all Legalist reform programs, these were designed to strengthen the power of the state and to

---

9   Zheng Liangshu鄭良樹, *A critical Biography of Shang Yang*《商鞅評傳》, Nanjing, Nanjing University Press, 2001.

10 Li Cunshan 李存山, *A critical Biography of Shang Yang: the reformer of Emperorism of Qin*《商鞅評傳──為秦開帝業的改革家》, Nanning, Guangxi Education Press, 1997, p.5.

enhance the authority of the sovereign.

Two stages were divided into the reform of Shang Yang. Firstly the stage was started in 356 B.C. when Shang Yang was officially becoming a powerful governor named Zuo Shu Zhang 左庶長.[11]　The main policies included:

　i　Encouragement of agriculture and suppression of commerce. 重農抑商

　ii　Rewarding military merits. 獎勵軍功

　iii　Banning　fights in private. 禁止私鬥

　iv　Reform of social structure. (Especially reform the official system) 二十等爵

The first reform achieved immediate success. And later he continued to launch the second reform. In 350 B.C., the chaotic warring situation among states was temporally stopped; Shang Yang kept on continuing his reform both economically and politically.[12] The second reform was based on the first reform and was advanced further. With a more fundamental reform and more systematic policies than the first reform, the second reform included :

　1. Moving the Qin capital to Xianyang. 遷都咸陽

　2. The promotion of the cultivation of wasteland. 開阡陌

　3. Establishment of the "Prefecture-County System", and elimination of the feudal fiefdom system. 行郡縣制[13]

11　Yang Kuan 楊寬, *Reforms of Shang Yang*《商鞅變法》, Shanghai, Shanghai Renmin Press, 1973, pp. 25-34.

12　Yang Kuan 楊寬, *Reforms of Shang Yang*《商鞅變法》, Shanghai, Shanghai Renmin Press, 1973, pp.35-42.

13　Cheung Wai Po 張偉保, Wen Rujia 溫如嘉, "Early Development of Prefecture and county System: taking Wei State as an Example"《郡縣制的早期發展：以魏國為中心》, Conference of the Memorial centenarian of Mr. Yan Gengwang 嚴耕望先生百齡紀念學術研討會, Hong Kong, Chinese University of Hong Kong, 2016.

4. Prohibition and division of big families. 小家庭為賦稅單位

5. Unification of weights and measures. 統一度量衡

6. Burning the *Shi*《詩》and the *Shu*《書》to clarify the Law.[14] 燔
《詩》《書》明法令

His reform also included the institution of collective guilt 連坐法, which launched mutual informing among the society; the enhancement of agriculture development and food production were called inducements; merchants' situation was worse by the further discrimination; prohibition of classical learning; abolishment of feudal fiefs; and by replacing the replaced local feudal power, the bureaucracy system of the state under the direct supervision of the central government was established.   After the two reforms by Shang Yang, the effects were remarkable: the Qin state became wealthy and powerful. The number of farmers, the area of arable land and the agriculture production all increased; the power of levying taxes became centralized, and the financial revenue increased; the customs and morals of the people improved; people became brave in fights and more cowardly in feuds for private interests, and the military strength of the state greatly increased.   All in all, as a result of these political reforms, the Qin state underwent drastic socio-economic and institutional changes and gained in strength both militarily   and economically.[15]

Like most legalist statist programs, the implementation of the reform of

---

14 *Han Fei Zi*《韓非子》, translated in to English by W.K.Liao, translated in to modern Chinese by Zhang Jue 張覺, Beijing, The Commercial Press, 2015, pp.238-247.

15 Cheung Wai Po 張偉保, Wen Rujia 溫如嘉, "Early Development of Prefecture and county System: taking Wei State as Centrality"《郡縣制的早期發展：以魏國為中心》, Conference of the Memorial centenarian of Mr. Yan Gengwang 嚴耕望先生百齡紀念學術研討會, Hong Kong, Hong Kong University, 2016.

Shang Yang was at the expense of aristocracy, who lost many prerogatives. It was under his dedication of planning and severe implementation that Qin, a half feudal and half nomadic state became a strong state.[16] Under his policy, Qin became strong within a few years and grew into a powerful state to further threaten the security of the states in the east of China.   Shang Yang incurred the wrath of prominent members of the nobility and the prince regent. After the death of Duke Xiao, Shang Yang lost the protection. Those nobles and the new ruler who were offended by his reform hunted him. And Shang Yang got executed by being torn to pieces by chariot pulling 五馬分屍 by the new ruler.

2.2.2.   The doctrine of Shang Yang

One textual history named *The Book of Lord Shang*《商君書》was now known by the people as one of the representatives of Legalist school.

The Book of Lord Shang is an anthology of the articles and sayings of Shang Yang and his disciples, and it is one of the classics of the Legalist school. The book is also called Shang Jun or Shang Zi. According to *the Han Shu*, the book Shang Jun included 29 Chapters[17]; however, there are only 24 Chapters:[18]

---

16 Zheng Liangshu鄭良樹, *A critical Biography of Shang Yang*《商鞅評傳》, Nanjing, Nanjing University Press, 2001.

17 〔Han〕Ban Gu〔漢〕班固, *Han Shu/History of the Former Han*《漢書》, Shanghai, Shanghai Guji Press, 12/2003, p1197.

18 〔Warring States〕Shang Yang〔漢〕商鞅, translated in to English Duyvendak J. J. L.; translated in to modern Chinese by Gao. Heng,*The Book of Lord Shang*, Beijing, The Commercial Press, 2006.

No.	Name	No.	Name
Chapter 1	The reform of the law 更法第一	Chapter 13	Making orders strict 靳令第十三
Chapter 2	An order of cultivating wastelands 墾令第二	Chapter 14	The cultivation of the right standard 修權第十四
Chapter 3	Agriculture and war 農戰第三	Chapter 15	The encouragement of immigration 徠民第十五
Chapter 4	The elimination of strength 去強第四	Chapter 17	Rewards of punishments 賞刑第十七
Chapter 5	Discussion about the people 說民第五	Chapter 18	Policies 畫策第十八
Chapter 6	The calculation of land 算地第六	Chapter 19	Within the borders 境內第十九
Chapter 7	Opening and debarring 開塞第七	Chapter 20	Weakening the people 弱民第二十
Chapter8	The unification of words 壹 言第八	Chapter 22	External and internal affairs 外內地二十二
Chapter 9	Establishing laws 錯法第九	Chapter 23	Prince and minister 君臣第二十三
Chapter 10	The method of warfare 戰法第十	Chapter 24	Interdicts and encouragements 禁使第二十四
Chapter 11	The establishment of fundamentals 立本第十一	Chapter 25	Attention to law 慎法第二十五
Chapter 12	Military defense 兵守第十二	Chapter 26	The fixing of right and duties 定分第二十六

Form 2.2.2 (1)

in the current version, those are divided into 5 volumes. Chapter 16 and Chapter 21 were lost.

There is a variety of argument of the authenticity of *The Book of Lord Shang*. The starter was a scholar named Huang Zhen 黃震 in Southern Song Dynasty, who expressed his doubts pointing out the structure of *The Book of Lord Shang* was different and chaotic.[19] After that, scholar Ma Duanlin 馬端臨 at the beginning of Yuan Dynasty, quoted some argument related to the authenticity of *The Book of Lord Shang* of *ZhouShi Shebi*《周氏涉筆》in his book *WenXian Tongkao*《文獻通考》, saying Shang Yang was not the only writer of *The Book of Lord Shang*.[20]In modern times, the argument of the authenticity of *The Book of Lord Shang* was continued and several scholars held that *The Book of Lord Shang* was written not just by Shang Yang but his followers were counted.[21][22][23] According to scholar Zheng Liangshu 鄭良樹, he considered that only Chapter 1: The reform of the law 更法第一; Chapter 2: An order to cultivate waste lands 墾令第二; Chapter 10: The method of warfare 戰法第十; Chapter 11: The establishment of

19 Huang Zhen黃震, *Huang Shi Ri Chao*《黃氏日抄》https://ctext.org/wiki.pl?if=gb&res=432683 卷五十五，"《商子》者，公孫商鞅之書也。始於《墾草》，……或疑鞅為法吏之有才者，其書不應煩亂若此，真偽殆未可知。"

20 〔Yuan〕Ma Duanlin〔元〕馬端臨, *Wen Xian Tong Kao*《文獻通考》, Beijing, Zhonghua Book Company, 1986, p. 1738.

21 Gao Heng 高亨, *Transliteration of Book of Shang Yang*《商君書註譯》, Beijing, Qinghua University Press, 2011.

22 Chen Qitian陳啟天, *Introduction of Chinese Legalist*《中國法家概論》, Beijing, Zhonghua Book Company, 1936.

23 Zheng Liangshu鄭良樹, *A critical Biography of Shang Yang*《商鞅評傳》, Nanjing, Nanjing University Press, 2001.

fundamentals 立本第十一; Chapter 12: Military defense 兵守第十二 and Chapter 19: Within the borders 境內第十九 were written by Shang Yang, others were written by the followers of Shang Yang. Although *The Book of Lord Shang* was not written by one person, we also considered it as a systematic doctrine base on the content of the book, which reflected the whole concept of the thought of Shang Yang. Furthermore, it reflected the development and reality of the school of Shang after the death of Shang Yang in that specific society.

With the full support of Duke Xiao, the Legalist program of social engineering designed by Shang Yang was very successful. It provided the strong military and economic bases that enabled the Qin state to unify China in later ages . Undoubtedly, Shang Yang was a strong supporter of "encouragement of agriculture and suppression of commerce".

According to his "An order to cultivate wastelands" of *The Book of Lord Shang*, we found that he made various policies to encourage agriculture. For the suppression of the merchant, a policy which both suppressed commerce and encouraged agriculture, the number of farmers would increase. To forbid people to buy commissariat, people have to grow their food instead. In the meanwhile, the policies of suppression of commerce also indirectly encouraged agriculture. Five policies related to the suppression of commerce were issued,[24] including 1. to forbid merchant to sell commissariat; 2.to increase the price of alcohol and meat; 3.no hotel; 4.to increase the commodity tax and 5. Servants of merchants had to perform military service.

---

24 Zheng Liangshu 鄭良樹, *Shang Yang and His School* 《商鞅及其學派》, Shanghai, Shanghai Guji Press, 1989, pp.169-181.

Furthermore, with the development of army and agriculture, people were settled down and remained in their proper sphere, trying to weaken the privilege of the aristocracy, and changing the society from slavery to bureaucracy was in need. With the reform of the establishment of the "Prefecture-County System 郡縣制", the more stable society of Qin state was shaped, and the Qin state was continually growing into a powerful situation. All thanks to the useful reform and the policies made by Shang Yang, he assisted the ruler to achieve the centralization of authority ata later time.

The time of Shang Yang was the time in a changing era from slavery to feudality. And the state of Qin was in the center of this transformation of society. Shang Yang used the power of landlords to weaken the privilege of the aristocracy. Many cases could be analyzed; however, the most typical one related to education was he made the policy to burn the Confucian classics. Once the Confucian classics were the representation of the upper class, what Shang Yang did to *Shi*《詩》 and *Shu*《書》, was helping the ruler to fool the people and made a way for everyone follow and only follow the Law that Legalist's school had drawn up. The "burn books and bury Confucian scholars" of the Qin dynasty was the later development of this policy.

2.3. Shen Buhai 申不害

Shen Buhai was a representative figure of Legalist' School during the Warring States period 戰國時期 known by his thought of Shu/Statecrafts 術. People also call him Shen Zi 申子.

2.3.1.   The biography of Shen Buhai

Shen Buhai (around 400 B.C. - 337 B.C.) was born in the Zheng state

鄭國. It was a chaotic time due to this complicated situation, and different thoughts of supporting the regulation, reformation, and development of the rulers. Shen Buhai was one of the officials which fit in the society. After the Han state 韓國 defeated the Zheng state 鄭國, the ruler of the sixth generation of Han state, Han Wu 韓武, also called Hou of Han Zhao 韓昭侯, appointed Shen Buhai as Chancellor of the Han state in charge of the social reform. According to *Shi Ji* 史記, Shen Buhai helped the Han state reformed the political structure and education system domestically, cooperated with other states nationally, and became a most strong and powerful state during his charge of 15 years.[25] In the meanwhile, when Sima Qian engaged in the discussion of the thoughts of Shen Buhai, he emphasized that the foundation of the thought of the Shen Zi was developed on the study of Huang Lao and mainly targeted on the technique called Xing Ming 申子之學本於黃老而主刑名.[26] The thought of Huang Lao was not described in detail; however, thanks to the comparative study of the handed-down documents and the newly excavated documents of Han silk book of Ma Wang Dui 馬王堆漢墓帛書, some scholars concluded it as the reformation of the original Taoist 道家思想 combined with other thoughts, especially the thoughts of Legalism and Confucianism with the main point of way 道, law 法, integrity 德.[27]Scholar Qian Mu 錢穆 said Shen Buhai was doing the academic work for the Duke of Han Zhao and being a chancellor for 15 years 學術以干韓昭

---

25 〔Han〕Sima Qian〔漢〕司馬遷, *Shi Ji/Records of the History*《史記》, Xuchang, Zhongzhou Guji Press, 1996, p. 612.

26 〔Han〕Sima Qian〔漢〕司馬遷, *Shi Ji/Records of the History*《史記》, Xuchang, Zhongzhou Guji Press, 1996, p. 612.

27 Zeng Zhenyu 曾振宇, "申不害術家說"再認識[J],《中國哲學史》, 1995(1):40-47

侯，相十五年.[28] His representative policy was known as Shu/Statecrafts 術. Shu/Statecrafts were a technique called Xing Ming Zhi Shu 形名之術. It formed self- attestation into 2 parts:

a. There were positions of the government, which try to appoint officials in a specific position according to his merits and capability. The merits and capabilities were called Xing 形 and the position and duties were called Ming 名. Statecrafts were the technique of Xing and Ming. This was part 1 of the self- attestation.

b. Once officials were put into positions using the technique of Xing and Ming, testing the capability of the officer to see if he did his work properly and to see if he was fit into his position, which   became part 2 of the self- attestation. It means the other part of statecraft was to test if Ming fitted the Xing.

It is hard to say this self- attestation of Xing Ming Zhi Shu created by Shen Buhai does not fit in the present   society when facing employee recruitment. That was the reason the Han state strived under the policy made by Chancellor Shen Buhai.

2.3.2.   The doctrine of Shen Buhai

There is not too much doctrine of Shen Buhai which remained in the handed-down documents. *Shi Ji* says there are 2 doctrines of Shen Buhai[29] and *History of the Former Han* says there are 6.[30] Actually, at present, only 1

---

28   Qina Mu 錢穆，《先秦諸子系年》，Beijing, The Commercial Press, 2015, pp.275-276.

29   〔Han〕Sima Qian〔漢〕司馬遷, *Shi Ji/Records of the History*《史記》, Xuchang, Zhongzhou Guji Press, 1996, p. 612.

30   〔Han〕Ban Gu〔漢〕班固, *Han Shu/History of the Former Han*《漢書》, Shanghai,

chapter named *Da Ti* 大體 can be found in Volume 36 of *Qun Shu Zhi Yao* 群書治要.

In *Da Ti*, Shen Buhai pointed out the importance of the rightfulness of the name. He said: with the rightfulness of the name/Ming 名, then the world could be ruled. Even the famous ruler Jie 桀 ruled the world with the rightfulness of the name/Ming 名. Once the name/Ming 名 (of the ruler) was wrongfulness, the world would be chaotic.[31] Ming 名 was repeatedly found in various handed-down documents related to Shen Buhai. This remaining trace may not be a selective and purposeful choice for the scholar, but the repetition would be read as a significant deduction for the core concept of the thought of Shen Buhai was Ming.[32] In the semi-late period of the Warring States period, the study of Ming was popular. Ming was not created by Shen Buhai, but he was the one who used this tactic to rule the state and had good outcomes. Shen Buhai was the peak of the study of Ming. He said many times about the rightfulness of the valuable Ming. The rightfulness of the Ming of Law was always the determinate of the face to rule society.[33]

2.4. Li Si 李斯

Li Si was more a practitioner than a scholar of Legalist teachings.

Shanghai Guji Press, 12/2003, p1196.

31 *Da Ti*《大體》：其名正，則天下治。桀之治天下也，亦以名。其名倚，而天下亂。

32 Xu Xiangmin 徐祥民, Shen Buhai's Thought of Law and Its Limitation申不害的法治思想及其局限性[J]，*Journal of Literature, History and Philosophy*《文史哲》，2003（2）：33-37.

33 Ma Teng 馬騰, On the Hsing － ming Theory and the Thought of Lawof Shen Pu － hai and Its Impact on Traditional Governance of Sovereignty申不害刑名法術思想及對傳統治道的影響[J]，*Tribune of Political Science and Law*《政法論壇》, 2015(6):76-86.

2.4.1. The biography of Li Si

Li Si (284 - 208 B.C.) was from Shangcai (上蔡) of Chu state. He was a junior official in his county when he was young.[34] After that, he learnt from the famous Confucian Xun Zi (荀子) about   how to rule. When he finished his education from Xun Zi, he found out that the opportunity to succeed in Chu state as an official was rare   and the other 5 states were weak, so he chose to move to the west and build up his political career in Qin state. Later on, Li Si became the chancellor, who   was the most powerful governor among the bureaucracy. He built up his political career step by step depending on his education of ruling and his skillfulness of using tactics.

He first served as a retainer in the family of Lv Buwei (呂不韋). After showing his capacity, Li Si got the chance to be a lobbyist, and then he became an official in Qin.   As an official of the Qin state, he was later promoted to be chancellor under Prince Yingzheng 嬴政 of Qin, and after this capable prince unified China and establish Qin Empire,   Li Si became a prime minister of the first Chinese imperial dynasty.

2.4.2. The influence of education from Li Si

Li Si was not a prolific writer. Only three of his short essays are preserved in *Shi Ji/Records of the History*《史記》. However, one of his policies impacted a great deal of education system during that time. It was "officials as teachers" 以吏為師. In the original text, it was written: during B.C. 213, the emperor of Qin Yingzheng started to burn all the books and

---

34 〔Han〕Sima Qian〔漢〕司馬遷, *Shi Ji/Records of the History*《史記》, Xuchang, Zhongzhou Guji Press, 1996, pp. 714-721. (*No.27 of Collected Biographies of Li Si* 《李斯列傳第二十七》)

commanded that "anyone who wants to learn, learn from the official".[35] This policy made an impact on the education system from the later legalist school and society. This policy determined whom people acknowledged and what exactly people could learn. In the meanwhile, in society during that period, this policy made by Li Si restrained the obligation for officials; being an official not only meant he had to govern the related issue, and he also had to make people acknowledgeable to related information, especially to the certain legal regulation.

When Qin was expanding rapidly, it needed more and more officials to govern the land and maintain the social order. During the Qin period, regardless of the change of official system, to be an official with a specific function for anyone of humble origins, the duration of learning was inevitable. . No matter which way he chose to learn, an official should be qualified and should be able to deal with certain issues.

2.5. Han Fei 韓非

"Intellectually, Han Fei was undoubtedly the greatest Legalist."[36]

2.5.1. The biography of Han Fei

Han Fei (280? – 233 B.C.) was an aristocracy of the Han state 韓國 in the late Warring States Period. Warring States Period was a critical turning period in history. Everything was changing during that time. It was changing

---

35 〔Han〕Sima Qian〔漢〕司馬遷, *Shi Ji/Records of the History*《史記》, Xuchang, Zhongzhou Guji Press, 1996, pp. 714-721.

36 Zhengyuan Fu, *China's Legalists the Earliest Totalitarians and Their Art of Ruling*, New York, M.E. Sharpe, 1996, p.20.

from feudal patrimonial system 分封制 to the prefecture-county system 郡縣制; it was changing from aristocracy 貴族制 to bureaucracy 官僚制; it was changing from the ruling of rites 禮治 to the ruling of laws 法治; it was changing from royal education 官學 to private education 私學. It was a crucial development period, and the doctrine of Han Fei played a part in the transformation of the society based on his thought that was fitted in the fluency of history.

Han state was surrounded by the powerful Qin 秦, Wei 魏 and Chu 楚 states in the late Warring States Period. During that time, it was obvious that the weak Han state would be integrated by other powerful states, and the inner domestic situation of the Han state was contiguous. Due the political corruption, Han Fei offered advice trying to make a reform to change this situation of Han state; however, his advice was not accepted by the sovereign. Han state sent Han Fei to Qin state as an ambassador, and Qin state used the strategy of Li Si 李斯, so Han Fei stayed in Qin State, and in the end, he passed away in Yun Yang.[37]

As a proficient writer, Han Fei stammered. His thought was appreciated by the sovereign of Qin state, Ying Zheng 嬴政, who unified China in 221 B.C. and established the Qin empire. According to *the Shi Ji*, Ying Zheng even said that "if I could meet him (Han Fei) and learn from him, I would die without regrets."[38] We could tell how much appreciation Ying Zheng gave to Han Fei. In 233 B.C., Han Fei was representing the Han state to visit Qin

---

37 〔Han〕Sima Qian 〔漢〕司馬遷, *Shi Ji/Records of the History*《史記》, Xuchang, Zhongzhou Guji Press, 1996, p.35.

38 〔Han〕Sima Qian 〔漢〕司馬遷, *Shi Ji/ Records of the History*《史記》, Xuchang, Zhongzhou Guji Press, 1996, pp. 611-613.

state as an envoy to ease the pressure of the military attack of Qin state. Ying Zheng was pleased to meet Han Fei. The admiration of Ying Zheng for Han Fei caused the envy of Li Si 李斯, for both Han Fei and Li Si studied from their teacher Master Xun Zi 荀子. Li Si was the minister of Qin court, and he convinced Ying Zheng that Han Fei was only loyal to his state and would not truly mean to give good advice to make Qin state better, so Han Fei was not trustworthy. Later on, Han Fei was arrested and put into prison. In the end, Han Fei was poisoned to death in the prison.[39]

Han Fei found a way to combine the three most useful political philosophies of Legalist's school including Laws 法, statecrafts 術 and positions 勢. It was one of the contributions that Han Fei made to the political philosophy. The unification of these elements is the core of the system of his thought. It was a great contribution to the Legalist's school. As a scholar well knowing how to rule, the work of Han Fei represented the most complete and comprehensive body of Legalist doctrines.[40] Han Fei built a systematic structural doctrine of his thought. He found that to use only one of them (Laws, statecrafts, and positions) could not govern the society well, so why not effectively use them to avoid the disadvantage and increase the effect of the advantage? These three elements in a certain way did compensate for each other. Scholar Jiang Chongyue in the Introduction of *Han Fei Zi* says that: "Han Fei considered that Laws can be used to make a country both

---

39 〔Han〕Sima Qian 〔漢〕司馬遷, *Shi Ji/Records of the History*《史記》, Xuchang, Zhongzhou Guji Press, 1996, pp. 611-613.

40 Zhengyuan Fu, *China's Legalists the Earliest Totalitarians and Their Art of Ruling*, New York, M.E. Sharpe, 1996, p.21.

strong and rich but cannot prohibit the viciousness of wicked ministers"[41];
"Statecrafts can be used to prohibit the viciousness of wicked minister"[42]
"but cannot strengthen a country".[43] "Laws and Statecrafts cannot be carried
out unless a sovereign owns his throne and holds   his power firmly. And
only when the sovereign knew well enough in suing Laws and Statecrafts can
keep his throne secure and the country peaceful and prosperous."[44] We agree
with the opinion of scholar Jiang Chongyue in that the conclusion of the three
most useful political philosophies of Han Fei helped the ruler of Pre-Qin and
Qin to conquer others and the education system based on the policy appeared
to be   the main reason for that implementation. .

2.5.2.   The work of Han Fei

According to *the Han Shu,* there were 55 chapters of *the Book Han Zi,*
which was also named *the Book Han Fei Zi.* A total of 55 chapters remain and
all of them are cohesive and the logic of writing from chapter to chapter is
clear. The contents of the book nearly cover all aspects of society.   In

---

41   〔Warring States〕Han Fei 〔戰國〕韓非, translated in to English by W.K.Liao, translated in to
modern Chinese by Zhang Jue張覺, *Han Fei Zi*《韓非子》, Beijing, The Commercial Press,
2015, pp.29 & 1672-1689.

42   〔Warring States〕Han Fei 〔戰國〕韓非, translated in to English by W.K.Liao, translated in to
modern Chinese by Zhang Jue張覺, *Han Fei Zi*《韓非子》, Beijing, The Commercial Press,
2015, pp. 29 &1770-1803.

43   〔Warring States〕Han Fei 〔戰國〕韓非, translated in to English by W.K.Liao, translated in to
modern Chinese by Zhang Jue張覺, *Han Fei Zi*《韓非子》, Beijing, The Commercial Press,
2015, pp. 29 & 1672-1689.

44   〔Warring States〕Han Fei 〔戰國〕韓非, translated in to English by W.K.Liao, translated in to
modern Chinese by Zhang Jue張覺, *Han Fei Zi*《韓非子》, Beijing, The Commercial Press,
2015, pp.29

accordance with *the Han Shu and* the doctrine we have today, we do not find any evidence that *the Book Han Fei Zi* or any of its chapters is missing.

The work of Han Fei was one of the Legalist's schools. Han Fei Zi has a variety of writing styles, such as arguments, persuasions, commentaries to classics, chins of pearls, and challenges.[45] The system of construction was an indispensable achievement of the book Han Fei Zi. In Han Fei's point of view, Laws, Statecrafts, and Positions were not completely identical.

i   Laws 法 in Han Fei's view were those written statutes. They were recorded and categorized in documents.

ii   Statecrafts 術 were a technique called Xing Ming Zhi Shu 形名之術. It could be divided into two parts. One was to appoint a suitable person as an official in a position according to his merits and capability. The merits and capabilities were called Xing 形 and the position and duties were called Ming 名. Statecrafts were the technique of Xing and Ming. Another part of statecraft was to test the capability of the officer to see if he did his work properly and to see if he was fit into his position. It means the other part of statecraft was to test if Ming fitted the Xing.

iiiPositions 勢 were not given a definite description by Han Fei. But we could tell from his work about what were positions.[46][47]

---

45 〔Warring States〕Han Fei〔戰國〕韓非, translated in to English by W.K.Liao, translated in to modern Chinese by Zhang Jue張覺, *Han Fei Zi*《韓非子》, Beijing, The Commercial Press, 2015, p.28.

46 https://zhidao.baidu.com/question/568908478.html?qbl=relate_question_0&word=%BA% AB% B7%C7%B7%A8%CA%F5%CA%C6

47 〔Warring States〕Han Fei〔戰國〕韓非, translated in to English by W.K.Liao, translated in to modern Chinese by Zhang Jue張覺, *Han Fei Zi*《韓非子》, Beijing, The Commercial Press,

Positions were the power of the throne. Laws, statecrafts, and positions all served   for the sovereign. Each of them had different emphases and functions. Laws were used to rule   commonplace, statecrafts to govern officials, and positions to defend the throne. The methods were different. The laws should be public to the people and the statecrafts should be used to rule the officers and remain secret, and positions were based on the natural power given to the throne, and it should be used basedon the combination of laws and statecrafts. The combination of Laws, statecrafts, and positions was not simply and adding them up together, Han Fei made it through the conclusion of previous Legalists, and it was a development of the theory of Legalist school.[48]

The ruling of laws was a direct crush of the aristocracy. In the slavery system, the punishment did not reach to the high officials because high officials are exempt from the penalties prescribed by the law 刑不上大夫,禮不下庶人.   The thought of Han Fei made a new path for the bureaucracy of the centralization of authority; it was ruptured from the slavery system of aristocracy during that time.[49]

Han Fei had an important theory to unify the laws, statecrafts, and positions. It was the nature of humans. Han Fei considered the human nature was egoistic 自私自利. In his point of view, human beings were selfish and were all trying to make a profit off them and trying to not be harmed by

---

2015, pp. 26-36, 44-47 (On the Difficulty in Speaking), 714-719 (Achievement and Reputation), 1634-1655 (A Critique of the Doctrine of Position) & 1804-1837 (Eight Canons).

48 Sun Kaitai 孫開泰, *A Brief History of Legalism in China*《法家史話》, Taipei, Kuo Chia Publishing Co., 2004, p.138.

49 Ren Jiyu 任繼愈, *Han Fei*《韓非》, Shanghai, Shanghai Renmin Press, 1964.

others 趨利避害, so, all the doctrines of Legalist's school he made were based on this opinion. Whether laws, statecrafts, or positions, they all made to use the egoism nature of human beings to control society. Laws were about punishment and reward, statecrafts were about scheme and stratagem, and positions were about ruling and domination. He used his doctrine to educate the ruler to make use of the egoistic feature of human nature and use laws to educate the people to obey the laws, otherwise,the consequence would come. In the doctrine of Han Fei, only the thrones make full use of the egoism of human nature can the law, statecrafts, and positions organically be implemented. In his doctrine, Han Fei repeatedly emphasized the ruling of laws 法治, the importance of agriculture and encouraging of military 耕戰 and weakening the power of the aristocracy and empowering the throne. He was sensitive of the float of history and accurately pointed out the conditions to teach the rulers and educate the society in his time.

Not too many things related to education were mentioned in Han Fei's doctrine, but we can explain his attitude about education from his thought.

In his book *Han Fei Zi* of Chapter 50 Learn Celebrities, he wrote: The intelligence of the people, like that of the infant, is useless... (民智之不可用，猶嬰兒之心也)， we could tell that, in the view of the legalist, the intelligence of common people was no more than infants who were never smart enough to be useful and were never capable of understanding their true interests. So education for that was not necessary and the only knowledge they should know was law so that the people would know what not to do in case they got punishment from the state. In the same book *Han Fei Zi* of Chapter 49 Five Vermin, he wrote: ...So, in the state ruled by the wise ruler, there was no classical literature, using Law as teaching education. It meant under the influence of legalist's school, the law was for the common people to learn and only law should be learned by people and other classical literature should be prohibited.

Undoubtedly, Han Fei Zi can be ranked as one of the masterpieces in the world for genuinely maintaining the sincere thought of the greatest Legalist thinker.[50]

2.6. The influence of Legalist school

It was Legalist School that helped the sovereign to build up the Qin Empire and to unify China. And the educational influence of legalist school: for common people, the policies legalist school made for them to learn were nothing but the law.

For general officers, because the policy of Li Si of officials as teachers, the general officer has to maintain a certain knowledge including characters, so that they can read the laws and teach them to the common people and learn other skills to suit in his position, which fits in the legalist thought of the technique of statecrafts.

The education influence of legalist school for the rulers was suited in the purpose of legalist school, to teach the ruler some knowledge so it can develop the revenue of the state, reinforce the power of the army, raise the output value of agriculture and facilitate the implementation of the rigid policies.

The Chinese imperial political tradition is described by most Chinese

---

50 〔Warring States〕Han Fei〔戰國〕韓非, translated in to English by W.K.Liao, translated in to modern Chinese by Zhang Jue張覺, *Han Fei Zi*《韓非子》, Beijing, The Commercial Press, 2015, p.35.

historians as "outside Confucian, inside Legalists 儒表法裏"; Chinese traditional official orthodox Confucianism was a mixture of classical Confucian rhetoric and legalist reinterpretation. Although the Chinese imperial dynastic era ended in 1911, the influence of the legalist tradition on Chinese development lasted more than 2300 years and can still exist today.

Chapter Three
Law as education (theoretical introduction)
以法為教（總論）

During Qin and Han dynasties, regardless of the changing of bureaucracy, a person came from a humble background but wanted to be an official, and to step into the officialdom, he had to learn certain knowledge to achieve the requirement of being an official. It did not matter whether those people receive their education through official school 官學, private school 私學, or learning from officials as trainees, and they had to meet the standards for professional competence.

Law School Study of Qin 秦律令學 is a well-studied topic; these studies are valuable for this topic. Since Qin followed the rule of "Law as education", learning the law of Qin is at a certain level learning the teaching materials of Qin. The newly excavated documents provide us with the precise materials. From the perspective of the completeness and quantity of the legal documents of Qin, *Qin bamboo slips of Yunmeng Shuihudi* are very impressive. *The Eighteen Qin Statutes*, *The statutes concerning Checking*, *The Miscellaneous Excerpts from Qin Statutes*, *The Answers to Questions Concerning Qin Statutes,* and *The Models for Sealing and Investigating* of Qin Law caused more concerns from the scholars of Law school study of Qin. Different versions of translation of *Qin Law of Qin bamboo slips of Yunmeng Shuihudi*, such as the Remnants of Ch'in Law,[1] were published. Other than

---

[1]   A.F.P. Huleswe, *Remnants of Ch'in Law: An Annotated Translation of the Ch'in Legal and*

translation, the analysis, and research of Law School Study of Qin were published as well. Scholars tried different ways to analyzethe law school study of Qin. Some of them scientifically organized the original excavated documents into the way that other people who have no background of paleography could read.[2] Some combined Qin Law and Legalist's School to do the research, trying to systematically describe the general theoretical principle of legalist through Qin Law and the legal practice of Qin.[3] Some separated the Qin Law into several topics for further discussion of the Law school study of Qin, trying to find out the relationship among Qin Law and its society, the punishment of Qin Law.[4] As mentioned above, Qin Law would be important for our study of teaching material of Qin, so, the research of Law School Study of Qin would be valuable.

In the meanwhile, except Law School Study of Qin, Law School Study of Han could be something to learn. In the Han dynasty, the chancellor Xiao made the Han Law based on the Qin Law. Even the Han Law failed to be handed down from past generations, and in 1983, more than 500 pieces of bamboo slips were found in the Han tomb of Zhangjiashan, Hubei. These Han bamboo slips were titled as *the Two-Year Laws*. The explanation of Two-

---

Administrative Rules of the 3rd Century B.C. Discovered in Yun-meng Prefecture, Hu-pei Province, in 1975, Leiden, E. J. Brill Publisher, 1985.

2 The organization team of bamboo slips of Qin tomb of Shuihudi 睡虎地秦墓竹簡整理小組, *Bamboo slips of Qin tomb of Shuihudi*《睡虎地秦墓竹簡》, Beijing, Cultural Relics Press, 1978.

3 Li Jin 栗勁, *The General Theory of Qin Law*《秦律通論》, Jinan, Shangdong Renmin publisher, 1985.

4 Cao Lvning曹旅寧, *New discovery of Qin Law*《秦律新探》, Beijing, China Social Sciences Press, 2002.

Year Law was studied.[5]   The relationship between Qin Law and Han Law was studied.[6]

3.1. What to learn?

Through the newly excavated documents and the documents handed down from ancient times, five types of teaching/learning materials could be categorized in the area of the education system of official-learn-to-be before the unification of Qin state. They included the textbook of laws and regulations, literacy textbooks, mathematic textbooks, and textbooks of official morality.

In *the bamboo slips of Yunmeng Shuihudi,* different kinds of content are written including *the Eighteen Qin Statutes, theChecking, and the Miscellaneous Experts from Qin Statutes, the Answers to Questions Concerning Qin Statutes, the Models for Sealing and Investigating, The Way to Be a Good Official, the Annals of mind* and so on. Only *the Chronological Record* was not involved in the teaching/learning materials for the education system of official-learn-to-be, the other nine could be considered as a group of materials that reflected some relatively complete information of the teaching/learning materials for the education system of official-learn-to-be. This is not ot far from that Shang Yang changed Fa into Lv 改法為律, and *the bamboo slips of Yunmeng Shuihudi* as an excavated document showed us

---

5 Zhu Honglin 朱紅林, *The Explanation Collection on the Two Year Laws of Zhangjiashan Bamboo Slips*《張家山漢簡〈二年律令〉》集釋, Beijing, Social Sciences Academic Press (China), 2005.

6 Wang Yanhui 王彥輝,*The Research of Han society and the Two Year Laws of Zhangjiashan*《張家山漢簡〈二年律令〉與漢代社會研究》, Beijing, Zhonghua Book Company, 2010. pp.1-4.

a complex picture of a society 2000 years ago with nearly 30 types of Lv/statutes covering a vast aspect of social life.[7]

The education system of official-learn-to-be 學吏制度 of Qin was first brought up in the book of the philosophers of the warring states. According to the difficulty of Bian He of *Han Fei Zi*《韓非子·和氏》,[8] it was written that Shang Yang taught Duke Xiao of Qin to burn the book of poetry and history and thereby make laws and orders clear.[9] The officials were those who understand laws, teach the meaning of the law to the public, and implement the thought of the ruler through laws. That made an official as a teacher in a certain way. Furthermore, according to the fixing of rights and duties of *the Book of Lord Shang*, it was written that "therefore the sages set up officers and officials for the laws and mandates, who should be authoritative in the empire, in order to define everyone's rights and duties, so that these are definite".[10] To set up the officials of laws as the teachers of the Qin state was in order to clarify the rights and duties. Not only did Lord Shang consider official to be the teacher of the public, but in the opinion of Han Fei he viewed affirmation of *law as education* and *officials as teachers*. All above

---

7 WU Shuchen 武樹臣, "Probe into the Cause ofChanging'Fa'into'Lu'in the Kingdom of Qin" 秦改法為律原因考 [J], *The Jurist*《法學家》, 2011(2): 28-40.

8 〔Warring States〕Han Fei〔戰國〕韓非, translated in to English by W.K.Liao, translated in to modern Chinese by Zhang Jue張覺, *Han Fei Zi*《韓非子》, Beijing, The Commercial Press, 2015, pp. 238-247.

9 〔Warring States〕Han Fei〔戰國〕韓非, translated in to English by W.K.Liao, translated in to modern Chinese by Zhang Jue張覺, *Han Fei Zi*《韓非子》, Beijing, The Commercial Press, 2015, p.245.

10 〔Warring States〕Shang Yang〔戰國〕商鞅, translated in to English Duyvendak J. J. L.; translated in to modern Chinese by Gao Heng,*The Book of Lord Shang*, Beijing, The Commercial Press, 2006.p.354.

are the views of the philosophers. However, if the thoughts were brought into practice, we were not sure about the outcome, due to the lack of documentary records. In the past, scholars usually took the *Shi Ji* as the authorized document and pointed out that the *officials as teachers* started on 213 B.C., which was the 34th year of the first emperor of Qin. On that year, the Qin government took the policy which was brought by the chancellor Li Si and promulgated by the empire about *officials as teachers*. From then on, *officials as teachers* officially became the education system of official-learn-to-be. Due to the fact that the newly excavated documents were found in recent years, especially, *Qin bamboo slips of Yunmeng Shuihudi* which was made after the reforms of Shang Yang and before the unification of Qin empire, they supplemented the related document, and we found from these newly excavated documents that the beginning of the *officials as teachers* was the way before 213 B.C. Thanks to the newly excavated documents, we could have a more complete picture of the education system of *officials as teachers.*

It was necessary to develop a group of qualified officials to deal with the daily management due to the huge number of miscellaneous affairs during the expansion of the Qin state. To raise proper officials became an issue and it was popular to learn to be an official during that time.

Before the unification of Qin Empire, there was public education 學室 set up by government; after the unification of Qin Empire, there was a line "anyone who wants to learn, learn from the official" ("有欲學者，以吏為師"). [11] This was a policy made by the chancellor of Qin, Li Si. However,

---

11 〔Han〕Sima Qian 〔漢〕司馬遷, *Shi Ji/Records of the History*《史記》, Xuchang, Zhongzhou Guji Press, 1996, p. 612.

in the newly excavated document of *Qin bamboo slips of Yunmeng Shuihudi*, before the unification of the Qin Empire, there was some policy related to "officials as teachers". One is in the statutes concerning the miscellaneous 內雜史 of *the Eighteen Qin statutes*, and it says: "if (persons) are not sons/students of clerks, they must not venture to study in the studyroom. Those who transgress this ordinance would have committed a crime 非史子也，毋敢學學室."[12] We can tell from this newly excavated document that, there was specialized study-room to train officials. The clerks were the officials who doing paperwork, archives work, and engrossment in government agencies at all levels. In the meanwhile, clerks also did the training work to develop disciples in this area. The archaeologist found various funeral objects in the grave of Xi 喜 and *Qin bamboo slips of Yunmeng Shuihudi*. And scholars believe that Xi was a Qin official who copied these large quantities of bamboo slips of Yunmeng Shuihudi. The clerks of the statutes concerning the miscellaneous of eighteen Qin statutes were part of the members of officials in the *officials as teachers*. The meaning of this bamboo slips is that only the sons/disciples of clerks could learn in the study-room. The teaching in the study-room mentioned above was handled with the tale in the hand of those qualified officials, which had professional proficiency and did what they teach in the study-room as routine work. The students, who study in the study-room, could begin their work as an assistant official after a certain time of learning and passing the qualifying examination.

---

12 A.F.P. Huleswe, *Remnants of Ch'in Law: An Annotated Translation of the Ch'in Legal and Administrative Rules of the 3rd Century B.C. Discovered in Yun-meng Prefecture*, Hu-pei Province, in 1975, Leiden, E. J. Brill Publisher, 1985.

Even more, not everyone could enter into the education system of official-learn-to-be and become an official. Those people with a criminal record were in the limitation and not allowed to be officials. We can tell this policy from *the bamboo slips of Yunmeng Shuihudi*: "Persons in detention who can write must not be made to engage in the work of clerks 下吏能書者，毋敢從史之事";[13] "Hou, robber guards, as well as the multitude of persons under detention one, should not venture to make assistants of clerks of government storehouses, as well as guards of Forbidden Parks 侯。司寇及群下吏毋敢為官府佐, 史及禁苑憲盜."[14]   These policies made sure the unobstructed way of official-to-be for the students who study in the study-room and led   people of official-want-to-be to learn in the regulatory place. And these policies made the management, training, and control of the students easier. Except these regulation found in *the bamboo slips of Yunmeng Shuihudi*, there was law specially equipped with the management of students named *the Statutes Concerning the Appointment of Retainers* 《除弟子律》. It was a law related to the management, development, and appointment of the students. Some regulation was kept in *the Miscellaneous Experts from Qin Statutes* 《秦律雜抄》 *the bamboo slips of Yunmeng Shuihudi*. The meaning of the original text[15] was discussed by varies scholars, and some said the

---

13 A.F.P. Huleswe, *Remnants of Ch'in Law: An Annotated Translation of the Ch'in Legal and Administrative Rules of the 3rd Century B.C. Discovered in Yun-meng Prefecture*, Hu-pei Province, in 1975, Leiden,   E. J. Brill Publisher, 1985, p.88.

14 A.F.P. Huleswe, *Remnants of Ch'in Law: An Annotated Translation of the Ch'in Legal and Administrative Rules of the 3rd Century B.C. Discovered in Yun-meng Prefecture*, Hu-pei Province, in 1975, Leiden,   E. J. Brill Publisher, 1985, p.88.

15 The organization team of bamboo slips of Qin tomb of Shuihudi 睡虎地秦墓竹簡整理小組, *Bamboo slips of Qin tomb of Shuihudi*《睡虎地秦墓竹簡》, Beijing, Cultural Relics Press, 1978.

meaning of the text was "when the students finish the study, his status as a student should be dismissed; he graduated but his student status did not be dismissed, and the official in charge of the student status should be punished"[16]. However, other scholars[17][18][19] had a second opinion of the original text. The research team of the bamboo slips of Yunmeng Shuihudi and scholar Hulsewé, A. F. P. thinks the meaning of the original text was "when (a person) is warranted to appoint retainers (but) the population register does not allow this, (or) when appointments are made carelessly, (such case) are all punished by shaving off the beard and being made a *Hou*."Even though there was a disagreement with the explanation of the original text, we could find in both explanations that there was registration/student status of the education system of official-learn-to-be in Qin. One thing could be pointed out in the education system of official-learn-to-be in Qin. Following the original text, it was said, "employment of one's retainers in excess (of the norms established by) the Statutes, as well as beating them, is fined one suit of armor; if the skin is broken (the fine is) two

---

16 Zhang Jinguang 張金光, *the Research of Qin's System*《秦制研究》, Shanghai, Shanghai Guji Press, 2004, p.711.

17 The organization team of bamboo slips of Qin tomb of Shuihudi 睡虎地秦墓竹簡整理小組, *Bamboo slips of Qin tomb of Shuihudi*《睡虎地秦墓竹簡》, Beijing, Cultural Relics Press, 1978.

18 A.F.P. Huleswe, *Remnants of Ch'in Law: An Annotated Translation of the Ch'in Legal and Administrative Rules of the 3rd Century B.C. Discovered in Yun-meng Prefecture*, Hu-pei Province, in 1975, Leiden, E. J. Brill Publisher, 1985

19 Li Qintong 李勤通, Zhou Dongping周東平, "Educational System of the Position of Officials at the Beginning of Qin and Han" 秦漢初期律令中的史官職業教育體系 [J], *Modern University Education*《現代大學教育》, 2016 (1):76-81.

suits of armor."[20]This means that, during that time, the retainers/officials could employ and even beat the students in the range of the law.

If a student could not finish his course, the consequence would be initiated. It was said that "when a coachman has been appointed for four years and he is unable to drive, the person who taught him is fined one shield, he is dismissed and he has to make good four years' statute labor and military service."[21]   We know that before the unification of the Qin Empire, all states were in a chaotic state of drastic wars, and the military service was rigorous and rigid.   In this document, we can tell that being a student could have an important advantage over other people. They could avoid military service. Only if the student did not achieve his course goal at a certain time would there be a consequence. Like the coachman in the text. That should be an attractive reason for people to enter the education system of official-learn-to-be.

There were civil and military officials during the period of the Qin and Han dynasties. Different kinds of officials had to learn different skills to approach their position.

The main task for officials of civil service was to deal with related paperwork so that the daily management could be run systematically and smoothly. Writing documents, hearing cases, making records, training students, and educating the public and other works were in the charge of

---

20 A.F.P. Huleswe, *Remnants of Ch'in Law: An Annotated Translation of the Ch'in Legal and Administrative Rules of the 3rd Century B.C. Discovered in Yun-meng Prefecture*, Hu-pei Province, in 1975, Leiden,   E. J. Brill Publisher, 1985, p.105.

21 The organization team of bamboo slips of Qin tomb of Shuihudi 睡虎地秦墓竹簡整理小組, *Bamboo slips of Qin tomb of Shuihudi*《睡虎地秦墓竹簡》, Beijing, Cultural Relics Press, 1978.

civil officials. The standards were as follows : firstly, the official had to know how to write based on "Persons in detention who are able to write must not be made to engage in the work of clerks".[22] This was the basic requirement. Secondly, civil officials had to be capable to deal with the civil affairs and thirdly was to understand the legal document. One was the position requirement to deal with cases; the other was to educate the public to make them understand the meaning of the legal statutes.

Xi was a typical case to tell what a civil official should learn and do. In the materials of *the Chronological Record*《編年紀》 in *the bamboo slips of Yunmeng Shuihudi*, we could see that Xi was a civil official engaging in legal education. He started his official position in the third year of Zheng 政, the ruler of Qin 三年,卷軍.八月,喜揄史. After one year, in the fourth year of ruler Qin Zheng, Xi was a low-level official named Yu Shi of Anlu (四年), □軍。十一月,喜□安陸□史. And at the sixth year of ruler Qin Zheng, Xi became an official of Ling Shi of Anlu 六年,四月,為安陸令史, which was a position as a subordinate of county magistrate in charge of the paperwork. Then next year, he was an official in Yang 七年,正月甲寅,鄢令史. At the twelfth year of ruler Qin Zheng, Xi was transferred to a position to rule the prison by judging cases in Yang 十二年,四月癸丑,喜治獄鄢. In this whole process, Xi was doing civil works related to document and case hearing. That might be the main reason Xi copied these great amounts of legal-related documents and buried them with himself .

According to the point of view of the ruling class, the education

---

22 A.F.P. Huleswe, *Remnants of Ch'in Law: An Annotated Translation of the Ch'in Legal and Administrative Rules of the 3rd Century B.C. Discovered in Yun-meng Prefecture*, Hu-pei Province, in 1975, Leiden, E. J. Brill Publisher, 1985, p.88.

system of official-learn-to-be was not only for the control of training officials and the passing on the knowledge of the laws to the public but also for the autocratic government to have full control of the culture education.

3.2. Legal learning materials

To further clarify the education system of official-learn-to-be, the teaching/learning materials at that time should be sorted out and categorized. As mentioned above, to adjust the urgent needs of centralized bureaucracy and to maintain a sufficient government, the sizable quantity of the requirement of officials caused the number of official-want-to-be to increase rapidly.   Therefore, the education of official-learn-to-be was popular. There must be materials to teach those students, and the government might have edited authoritative teaching/learning materials.

In terms of the content of *the bamboo slips of Yunmeng Shuihudi*, except *The Chronological Record* and *the daily book* 《日書》, the rest are all directly related to the education system of official-learn-to-be and among them some are the typical legal learning materials.

Because *the bamboo slips of Yunmeng Shuihudi* was discovered in the grave of Xi, we could reasonably assume that these excavated documents of laws and regulations were selected works of Xi and they did not cover   the whole legal system.

Some scholars argued that the research of those excavated documents could be reliable   if those documents essentially copied   from laws made by the central government during that time, or just contents altered or changed simply based on personal choice.[23] However, even though *the*

---

23 〔日〕廣瀨薰雄,《秦漢律令研究》,汲古書院,2009, p.10.

*bamboo slips of Yunmeng Shuihudi*did not likely strictly copy from laws, it still had major value for research , as a group of learning material for the official-learn-to-be during that time. No matter the kinds of laws or the content of each kind of law, they could not possibly be the overall law system statutes. One strong proof was that within *the Eighteen Qin Statutes,* one group of bamboo slips was statutes that concern *theChecking*《效律》, and there was another group of bamboo slips found from a different place of the same tomb, which was called *the Statutes Concerning Checking*《效律》. These two groups bamboo slips were all related to the laws of checking. However, *the Checking*, which was included in *the Eighteen Qin Statutes,* was a selected version of *The Statutes Concerning Checking.* There were 8 statutes of *Checking* of *the Eighteen Qin Statutes*, and all of the 8 statues were overlapped with the content of part of *the Statutes concerning Checking.*This means that *the Checking*, as a group of statutes with *the Eighteen Qin Statute,* was not the complete regulation of the checking issue; however, it was simply a selected version of *the Statutes Concerning Checking.* Comparing this case with all the content of *the Eighteen Qin Statutes*, the Eighteen Qin Statutes might have been a selected part of the legal structure of Qin. Each part of *the Eighteen Qin Statutes* could be a selected version of the regulations of the legal system. We had no idea why the one (likely Xi or the people related to Xi) who chose these statutes and combined them as the *Eighteen Qin Statute;*however, we could tell this gave us a good glimpse to look at the whole picture of the legal system of Qin and it was valuable for us to learn the education system of official through these materials.

These selected works of legal materials should be deeply concerned with

Xi's work or daily routine. With so many documents buried with Xi, and from the size of the grave and numbers of the funeral objects, Xi should be at least an official in Qin.[24] Or at least we could tell that Xi was born in a family of officials.[25] All the documents that buried with him were related to law enforcement, and with the specialty of these excavated documents, we could deduce that they were the selected version of legal learning materials for certainty.

---

24 The organization team of bamboo slips of Qin tomb of Shuihudi 睡虎地秦墓竹簡整理小組, *Bamboo slips of Qin tomb of Shuihudi*《睡虎地秦墓竹簡》, Beijing, Cultural Relics Press, 1978. P.12 & 107.

25 Huang　Liuzhu　(黃留珠, 1983)黃留珠, "Shi Zi, Study Room and Xi Yu Shi: Reading Note of Qin bamboo slips of Yunmeng Shuihudi" "史子"、"學室"與"喜揄史"——讀雲夢秦簡劄記[J], *The Journal of Humanities (Bimonthly)*《人文雜志》,1983(2).

Chapter Four
Law as education (substantial contents)
以法為教（分論）

4.1. *The Eighteen Qin Statutes*《秦律十八種》

There were 201 bamboo slips of *The Eighteen Qin Statutes* 《秦律十八種》and all of them were placed on the right side of the body of the tomb owner. There were names or shorted form of titles at the end of each statute. [1] Within these legal learning materials buried with Xi, there were 108 items/articles of *the Eighteen Qin Statutes.* The content of it was wildly involved with many aspects of society in Qin, from knowing how to run the institution of minority nationality such as *the statutes concerning the Dependent states* 《屬邦》[2] to checking penal statutes such as *the statutes concerning the Commandant; Miscellaneous* 《尉雜》.[3] It showed us that different officials would have the chance to manage a variety of different social life in a complicated way. The things and skills for an official-learn-to-be were not easy.

1　The organization team of bamboo slips of Qin tomb of Shuihudi 睡虎地秦墓竹簡整理小組, *Bamboo slips of Qin tomb of Shuihudi*《睡虎地秦墓竹簡》, Beijing, Cultural Relics Press, 1978. p.23.

2　A.F.P. Huleswe, *Remnants of Ch'in Law: An Annotated Translation of the Ch'in Legal and Administrative Rules of the 3rd Century B.C. Discovered in Yun-meng Prefecture*, Hu-pei Province, in 1975, Leiden, E. J. Brill Publisher, 1985. pp91-92.

3　A.F.P. Huleswe, *Remnants of Ch'in Law: An Annotated Translation of the Ch'in Legal and Administrative Rules of the 3rd Century B.C. Discovered in Yun-meng Prefecture*, Hu-pei Province, in 1975, Leiden, E. J. Brill Publisher, 1985. p.90.

In *the Eighteen Qin Statutes,* a variety of social aspects were   discussed, and it taught about agriculture such as *the Statutes on Agriculture* 《田律》 with total 6 statutes,[4] and the official-in-charge had to file a report about the harvest and damage situation of crops. People should be rewarded for knowing how to raise livestock and be punished for mistreatment   by the statutes.[5] It is reported   that officials should report the detail of corps and cultivate fields and monitor the situation of floods, hordes of grasshoppers, or other damage to the crops. It was selected as the first statutes by Xi. The first three groups of statutes were all related to farming, farm animals, and the storage of corps[6], with a total of 25 statutes, which were all about agriculture. We could tell how important agriculture could be during that time. And making sure the agriculture went smoothly was an indispensable thing for the officials' daily management, so they should be taught about the importance of it when they were in the official training.   *The statutes on Currency*《金布律》 with total 15 statutes[7] and *the statutes on Passes and Market*   《關市》 with only 1 statute[8] regulated the translation of currency and trading of the

---

4   A.F.P. Huleswe, *Remnants of Ch'in Law: An Annotated Translation of the Ch'in Legal and Administrative Rules of the 3rd Century B.C. Discovered in Yun-meng Prefecture,* Hu-pei Province, in 1975, Leiden,   E. J. Brill Publisher, 1985. pp.21-25.

5   A.F.P. Huleswe, *Remnants of Ch'in Law: An Annotated Translation of the Ch'in Legal and Administrative Rules of the 3rd Century B.C. Discovered in Yun-meng Prefecture,* Hu-pei Province, in 1975, Leiden,   E. J. Brill Publisher, 1985. pp.26-29

6   A.F.P. Huleswe, *Remnants of Ch'in Law: An Annotated Translation of the Ch'in Legal and Administrative Rules of the 3rd Century B.C. Discovered in Yun-meng Prefecture,* Hu-pei Province, in 1975, Leiden,   E. J. Brill Publisher, 1985. pp.21-245.

7   A.F.P. Huleswe, *Remnants of Ch'in Law: An Annotated Translation of the Ch'in Legal and Administrative Rules of the 3rd Century B.C. Discovered in Yun-meng Prefecture,* Hu-pei Province, in 1975, Leiden,   E. J. Brill Publisher, 1985. pp.46-55.

8   A.F.P. Huleswe, *Remnants of Ch'in Law: An Annotated Translation of the Ch'in Legal and

market. *The statutes on Passes and Market* noted the way of transaction. It would be fined one suit of armor if the workshops 作務 and government storehouse were not seen to enter the cash into money-box. It was regulated in such a detailed way, and we could tell the regulation was closely associated with every aspect of life to the people.

There were 6 statutes of *the Statutes on Artisans* 《工律》,[9] 3 statutes of *the Statutes on Norms for Artisans* 《工人程》[10] and 3 statutes of *the Statutes on Equalization Artisans* 《均工》.[11] All of them were regulation in different aspects of artisans. The first statute of *the Statutes on Artisans* said that when making vessels of the same type, their size, length, and width should also be identical. It was a statute for the regulation of the standards of vessels. We say that the unification of currency and weights and measures is a great contribution the Qin Empire had made . *The Statutes on Artisans* of *the Eighteen Qin Statutes* could be taken as one of the steps to achieve this goal through the legal system. One interesting fact found in *the Statutes on Norms for Artisans* was that it reflected the process production level at that

---

Administrative Rules of the 3rd Century B.C. Discovered in Yun-meng Prefecture, Hu-pei Province, in 1975, Leiden, E. J. Brill Publisher, 1985. p.56.

9 A.F.P. Huleswe, *Remnants of Ch'in Law: An Annotated Translation of the Ch'in Legal and Administrative Rules of the 3rd Century B.C. Discovered in Yun-meng Prefecture*, Hu-pei Province, in 1975, Leiden, E. J. Brill Publisher, 1985. pp.57-60.

10 A.F.P. Huleswe, *Remnants of Ch'in Law: An Annotated Translation of the Ch'in Legal and Administrative Rules of the 3rd Century B.C. Discovered in Yun-meng Prefecture*, Hu-pei Province, in 1975, Leiden, E. J. Brill Publisher, 1985. p.61.

11 A.F.P. Huleswe, *Remnants of Ch'in Law: An Annotated Translation of the Ch'in Legal and Administrative Rules of the 3rd Century B.C. Discovered in Yun-meng Prefecture*, Hu-pei Province, in 1975, Leiden, E. J. Brill Publisher, 1985. p.62.

time. Winter could be less productive than summer[12], women doing labor work could be less productive[13] than men but in terms of doing needlework, woman and man should be equally productive[14]. It should be pointed out was that we did not know the statute related to the equivalent of the workload for woman and man, saying "two bond-women is equivalent to that of one artisan. Four bond-women taking their turn of duty is equivalent to that of one artisan", [15] was regulated based on physiological similarities and differences between men and women, or it was simply based on the job differentiation or social class. As far as the author concerned, this regulation was mainly made by physiological similarities and differences. During that period, the labor work was heavy, and men were averagely stronger than women, so two bond-women are equivalent to that of one artisan-made sense. Meanwhile, in terms of the needlework, which women was good at, in comparison with the artisan who was good at it, the workloads for both women and men were the same.[16]

---

12 A.F.P. Huleswe, *Remnants of Ch'in Law: An Annotated Translation of the Ch'in Legal and Administrative Rules of the 3rd Century B.C. Discovered in Yun-meng Prefecture*, Hu-pei Province, in 1975, Leiden, E. J. Brill Publisher, 1985. p.61.

13 A.F.P. Huleswe, *Remnants of Ch'in Law: An Annotated Translation of the Ch'in Legal and Administrative Rules of the 3rd Century B.C. Discovered in Yun-meng Prefecture*, Hu-pei Province, in 1975, Leiden, E. J. Brill Publisher, 1985. p.61.

14 A.F.P. Huleswe, *Remnants of Ch'in Law: An Annotated Translation of the Ch'in Legal and Administrative Rules of the 3rd Century B.C. Discovered in Yun-meng Prefecture*, Hu-pei Province, in 1975, Leiden, E. J. Brill Publisher, 1985. p.61.

15 A.F.P. Huleswe, *Remnants of Ch'in Law: An Annotated Translation of the Ch'in Legal and Administrative Rules of the 3rd Century B.C. Discovered in Yun-meng Prefecture*, Hu-pei Province, in 1975, Leiden, E. J. Brill Publisher, 1985. p.61.

16 A.F.P. Huleswe, *Remnants of Ch'in Law: An Annotated Translation of the Ch'in Legal and Administrative Rules of the 3rd Century B.C. Discovered in Yun-meng Prefecture*, Hu-pei Province, in 1975, Leiden, E. J. Brill Publisher, 1985. p.61.

The Statute on Labor《徭律》[17] of *The Eighteen Qin Statutes* was a regulation forcing plebeian to do corvee. Doing corvee was a typical form for the feudalism to oppress and exploit plebeian. And writing it in the legal system could efficiently send a message to the public about how they should do their labor to serve the upper class/state, and it could be called　education of enslavement. The main corvee was the construction work, and the plebeians that were forced to do those labors always faced　physical and monetary punishment. *The Controller of Works* 《司空》with 13 statutes[18] further guaranteed the implementation of corvee. If people were in debt and could not repay in time, he would be forced to do corvee in return. *The Statutes concerning the controller of Works* listed many penalties and punishments; however, even those who work off fines, redemption fees or debts, could have days off on the occasion of agriculture for sowing and weeding.[19]   Scholar Hulsewé in his book[20] considered that "二旬" of the statute in t*he Statutes concerning the controller of Works* is "2 decades",[21] whose original text　is: "Persons who work off fines, redemption

---

17 A.F.P. Huleswe, *Remnants of Ch'in Law: An Annotated Translation of the Ch'in Legal and Administrative Rules of the 3rd Century B.C. Discovered in Yun-meng Prefecture*, Hu-pei Province, in 1975, Leiden,　E. J. Brill Publisher, 1985. pp.63-65.

18 A.F.P. Huleswe, *Remnants of Ch'in Law: An Annotated Translation of the Ch'in Legal and Administrative Rules of the 3rd Century B.C. Discovered in Yun-meng Prefecture*, Hu-pei Province, in 1975, Leiden,　E. J. Brill Publisher, 1985. pp.66-75.

19 A.F.P. Huleswe, *Remnants of Ch'in Law: An Annotated Translation of the Ch'in Legal and Administrative Rules of the 3rd Century B.C. Discovered in Yun-meng Prefecture*, Hu-pei Province, in 1975, Leiden,　E. J. Brill Publisher, 1985. pp.66-75.

20 A.F.P. Huleswe, *Remnants of Ch'in Law: An Annotated Translation of the Ch'in Legal and Administrative Rules of the 3rd Century B.C. Discovered in Yun-meng Prefecture*, Hu-pei Province, in 1975, Leiden,　E. J. Brill Publisher, 1985.

21 A.F.P. Huleswe, *Remnants of Ch'in Law: An Annotated Translation of the Ch'in Legal and*

fees or debts return (home) for agricultural work at the time of sowing and at the time of weeding, on both (occasions) two decades." which as far as I am concerned, it should be 20 days instead of 2 decades. Because normally the sowing or weeding would not last longer than an agriculture season per year, giving those who work off fines and debts 20 years for helping sow and weed at home would not make sense to implement the punishment. "20 days off" would be more reasonable to explain the statute during that period of Qin.

The word of Aristocratic Rank for Military Action "軍爵" was first seen in the Chapter *within the Borders* 《境內》 of *The Book of Lord Shang*《商君書》. *The Statutes Concerning Aristocratic Rank for Military Action* 《軍爵律》 of *The Eighteen Qin Statutes* was 2 written regulations.[22] One regulated the situation to and not to give an aristocratic rank of the military award; the other regulated the usage to trade with the aristocratic rank of the military award.

There were 3 statutes of *the Statutes concerning the Establishment of Officials*《置吏律》[23]of *the Eighteen Qin Statutes.* They regulated when and how to establish officials and how to deal with the absence of officials.

Administrative Rules of the 3rd Century B.C. Discovered in Yun-meng Prefecture, Hu-pei Province, in 1975, Leiden, E. J. Brill Publisher, 1985, p.67.

22 A.F.P. Huleswe, *Remnants of Ch'in Law: An Annotated Translation of the Ch'in Legal and Administrative Rules of the 3rd Century B.C. Discovered in Yun-meng Prefecture*, Hu-pei Province, in 1975, Leiden, E. J. Brill Publisher, 1985. p.82.

23 A.F.P. Huleswe, *Remnants of Ch'in Law: An Annotated Translation of the Ch'in Legal and Administrative Rules of the 3rd Century B.C. Discovered in Yun-meng Prefecture*, Hu-pei Province, in 1975, Leiden, E. J. Brill Publisher, 1985. pp.76-77.

There were 8 statutes of *the Checking*《效》[24]of *the Eighteen Qin Statutes.* There were rules to verify and check the asset of the government. They were mainly about who, how, and what to check the granary.

There were 3 statutes of *the Statutes concerning the Rations for Holders of Passports*《傳食律》[25]of *the Eighteen Qin Statutes.* The proportion and ration of food supply to certain officials was written in this group of statutes.

As to how to send and receive the legal document, there were 2 *Statutes concerning the Forwarding of Documents*《行書》[26] of *the Eighteen Qin Statutes* which had been found.

If we said the above statutes were related to officials who daily manage and govern the society, then, *the Statutes Concerning the Minister; Miscellaneous*《內史雜》[27] was a group of regulations related to how to manage and governing officials themselves. It regulated that all the applicable law should be copied by the general officials of each prefecture.[28] Even it

---

24 A.F.P. Huleswe, *Remnants of Ch'in Law: An Annotated Translation of the Ch'in Legal and Administrative Rules of the 3rd Century B.C. Discovered in Yun-meng Prefecture*, Hu-pei Province, in 1975, Leiden, E. J. Brill Publisher, 1985. pp.87-81.

25 A.F.P. Huleswe, *Remnants of Ch'in Law: An Annotated Translation of the Ch'in Legal and Administrative Rules of the 3rd Century B.C. Discovered in Yun-meng Prefecture*, Hu-pei Province, in 1975, Leiden, E. J. Brill Publisher, 1985. pp.83-84.

26 A.F.P. Huleswe, *Remnants of Ch'in Law: An Annotated Translation of the Ch'in Legal and Administrative Rules of the 3rd Century B.C. Discovered in Yun-meng Prefecture*, Hu-pei Province, in 1975, Leiden, E. J. Brill Publisher, 1985. p.85.

27 A.F.P. Huleswe, *Remnants of Ch'in Law: An Annotated Translation of the Ch'in Legal and Administrative Rules of the 3rd Century B.C. Discovered in Yun-meng Prefecture*, Hu-pei Province, in 1975, Leiden, E. J. Brill Publisher, 1985. pp.86-89.

28 A.F.P. Huleswe, *Remnants of Ch'in Law: An Annotated Translation of the Ch'in Legal and Administrative Rules of the 3rd Century B.C. Discovered in Yun-meng Prefecture*, Hu-pei Province, in 1975, Leiden, E. J. Brill Publisher, 1985. pp.86-89.

did not tell the reason for coping with the law, it was not hard to tell how it benefited the society in the education way. This reflected that the regulation forced the official to copy the applying law, to a certain degree; they would categorize the law, and run them logically and understandably. On the other hand, this regulation made it easier to imply the rule of "law as education" 以法為教. Furthermore, *the Statutes Concerning the Minister; Miscellaneous* revealed the educational background of a qualified official. Firstly, the sinners must not work in the government;[29] even they might be educated and could write.[30] Secondly, only the sons of the clerks could study in the study-room, otherwise, there would be punishment.[31] We could see that some of the government positions were passed on generation by generation. As the statute said, only the sons of clerks could study in the study-room, and after the sons of clerks finish their education in the study-room, they could become officials. So, we could tell at least the position of the clerk was passed on generation by generation. Lastly, as we discussed above, there wasa private way to receive education 私學, which was to study from the master, and there was a public way to receive education 官學, which was to study in the study-room as the statute mentioned. Here we pointed out that if persons

---

29 A.F.P. Huleswe, *Remnants of Ch'in Law: An Annotated Translation of the Ch'in Legal and Administrative Rules of the 3rd Century B.C. Discovered in Yun-meng Prefecture*, Hu-pei Province, in 1975, Leiden, E. J. Brill Publisher, 1985. pp.86-89.

30 A.F.P. Huleswe, *Remnants of Ch'in Law: An Annotated Translation of the Ch'in Legal and Administrative Rules of the 3rd Century B.C. Discovered in Yun-meng Prefecture*, Hu-pei Province, in 1975, Leiden, E. J. Brill Publisher, 1985. pp.86-89.

31 A.F.P. Huleswe, *Remnants of Ch'in Law: An Annotated Translation of the Ch'in Legal and Administrative Rules of the 3rd Century B.C. Discovered in Yun-meng Prefecture*, Hu-pei Province, in 1975, Leiden, E. J. Brill Publisher, 1985. pp.86-89.

were not the sons of clerks, they must not venture to study in the studyroom. The Han dynasty carried forward accede from Qin empire, in *the Statutes of Commandant*《尉律》of Han dynasty, which quoted by Xu Shen 許慎 in his book *First Chinese Dictionary*/Shuo Wen Jie Zi《說文解字·敘》. It said that to be an official of paperwork/document, there were standards to meet; one was to be at least 17 years old, and the other was to become literate of 9000 characters.[32] If both statutes reflected the practical situation during that time, it meant that to become an official, the education process of the person could be receiving education through the study-room, of which the teachers were officials, if he was the son of a clerk and at least becoming literate of 9000 characters. *The Statutes Concerning the Minister of Finance; Miscellaneous* was closely related tothe education of the system of official-learn-to-be.

The Eighteen Qin Statutes were statutes related to the rules from the central government, the affairs of central and local governments , the relationship between states and minorities, and the actual governing of the officials. The focuses of the selected materials of Xi were the actual government of the lower-level officials, and these focuses were exactly the right educational materials for the basic learning to the official-learn-to-be.

4.2. *The Answers to Questions Concerning Qin Statutes*《法律問答》

There were 210 bamboo slips of *the Answers to Questions Concerning Qin Statutes* 《法律問答》and were placed on the right side of the neck of the tomb owner Xi. This group of bamboo slips gave certain interpretations/

---

32 The further research of the teaching materials of literacy would be discussed in chapter 5.

explanations to a few statutes, terms, and intentions with the mode of Questions and Answers.[33] It is historically valuable for us to understand the legal system and society of Qin. After the political reform of Shang Yang 商 鞅變法, the Qin state implied the policy of "the fixing of the right standard is decided by the prince 權制獨斷於君", in which we could find the document was written in *the Cultivation of the Right Standard* 修權第十四.[34] The laws of Qin were made by the ruler and there were officials who specialized in interpreting those laws. According to this, t*he Answers to Questions Concerning Qin Statutes* should be legally binding at that time and would not be written by random people. To the content of the documents, if we said that *the Eighteen Qin Statutes,* which included civil laws, procedure laws, criminal laws, and administrative laws, was a complex combination of the reflection of the legal system, then, *the Answers to Questions Concerning Qin Statutes* more stick to criminal laws which the officials-to-be to learn in the education aspect and they imply in the trail system. It included 190 statutes.[35] In the *Bamboo slips of the Qin tomb of Shuihudi,* it writes that there are 187 statutes of the Answers to Questions concerning Qin Statutes, and after counting the statutes, we know the actual number is 190. So, number 187 may be a written mistake. [36] It mostly answered those questions

---

33 The organization team of bamboo slips of Qin tomb of Shuihudi 睡虎地秦墓竹簡整理小組, *Bamboo slips of Qin tomb of Shuihudi*《睡虎地秦墓竹簡》, Beijing, Cultural Relics Press, 1978. p.149.

34 Gao Heng 高亨, *Transliteration of Book of Shang Yang*《商君書註譯》, Beijing, Qinghua University Press, 2011. P. 208-209.

35 Li Junming李均明, *Organization and Analysis of the text of strips of Qin and Han*《秦漢簡牘文書分類輯解》, Beijing, Cultural Relics Press, 2009.

36 The organization team of bamboo slips of Qin tomb of Shuihudi 睡虎地秦墓竹簡整理小組,

related to penalty reduction and sentence extension. The statutes involved the interpretation of the laws of robbery, murder, marriage, joining army, census registry, fighting, and slavery and so on, and among them the biggest portion was theft. There were 42 statutes related to theft in *the Answers to Questions concerning Qin Statutes.*

In the education way, it was another learning material for the official-learn-to-be. It explained the criminal law of Qin, which was the main content of law during that time. As we knew, Shang Yang made law according to *the Fa Jing* of Li Kui, which separated all the content into Law of Rob 《盜法》, Law of Thief 《賊法》, Law of Imprison 《囚法》, Law of Arrest 《捕法》, Law of Za《雜法》 and Law of Ju 《具法》. The scope of *the Answers to Questions Concerning Qin Statutes* was similar to the categorization of *the Fa Jing*. Even it was found lying scattered, the organization team of bamboo slips of Qin tomb of Shuihudi arranged this group of bamboo slips in the way of the 6 chapters of the *Fa Jing*.

The main content of the Questions was those laws applied in the period of Duke Xiao of Qin 秦孝公, and the Answers were mainly made during the period of Duke Hui of Qin 秦惠王 or the Dukes afterward. The way to write *the Answers to Questions Concerning Qin Statutes* was extremely like the legal interpretation of the court in comparison with the present day. There were many parts which cited the Ting Xing Shi 廷行事, which was the legal precedent formed during trials. There were 7 statutes which mentioned Ting Xing Shi. Some of the situation of the statutes were irrelevant because they

---

Bamboo slips of Qin tomb of Shuihudi《睡虎地秦墓竹簡》, Beijing, Cultural Relics Press, 1978, p.149.

were not direct legislation to support it, but the judge chose to use those cases as an exception rather than follow the laws 以例破律. It showed us that there was no strict limitation for the interpretation like *the Answers to Questions concerning Qin Statutes*.[37] Ting Xing Shi could be the legislative authority which reflected the choice made by the officials, and as we could see the total amount of them, it reflected a comprehensive legal system of criminal laws at that time. This kind of legal interpretation represented that law was not a tool to strictly bound the feudal rulers, but a tool to suppress the labor, plebeian and public, based on the fact that the official could choose to follow the statutes or the legal precedent from other courts, no matter whether there were or statutes or no in writings. The judging official could apply the laws in a wide range.

It was not very long after the society transited from slavery to feudality, and the laws of Qin showed the mind of feudalism and tried to suppress the development of slavery.[38] Even though we said the laws of Qin mainly protect the feudal rulers and upper class, we found a very distinguished thing in *the Answers to Questions concerning Qin Statutes*. It was also an academic discussion. The original content was: "…The household is 'those who dwell together'. Servants are adjudicated, for servants' the household is

---

37 Chen Rui 陳銳, Gao Yuan 高袁, A Kind of Simple Technique: Legal Interpretation Method in"the Asks and Answers to Law Written in the Bamboo Slips Found in the Qin Dynasty Tomb" 素樸的技巧：《法律問答》中的法律解釋方法 [J], *Zheng Fa Lun Cong* 《政法論叢》, 12/2011 (6)：60-65.

38 Li Mingxiao 李明曉, The Study of Laws in Bamboo Slips Excavated from Ancient Tombs of the Qin Dynasty in Shuihudi 《睡虎地秦墓竹簡》法律用語研究[D], Chongqing, Southwest China Normal University, 04/2003.

not adjudicated 戶為同居, 坐隸, 隸不坐戶謂."[39] The explanation of the Organization team of *The Bamboo Slips of Qin Tomb of Shuihudi* said it meant that, if a slave committed a crime, the owner should also be punished; on the other hand, if the owner committed a crime, the slave did not have to be punished.[40] However, some scholars had a different opinion. [41] They said that it should be explained in this way: if the slave committed a crime, the owner should not be punished; the owner committed a crime, the slave should have to be punished. Lots of pieces of evidence were displaced in the article and sparked an academic discussion. As far as I am concerned, I agreed to the second explanation. In all the slavery history, the slave is always the one being punished and the slave owner could get rid of punishment or keep his slave punished in hisplace. There was no way that the Qin law dispensing justice in a way that did not fit the existingsituation of the society.

4.3. *Miscellaneous Excerpts from Qin Statutes* 《秦律雜抄》

There were 42 bamboo slips of *the Miscellaneous Excerpts from Qin Statutes* 《秦律雜抄》 and were placed under the belly of the tomb owner Xi. It was a group of bamboo slips with a complex form including some with

---

39 The organization team of bamboo slips of Qin tomb of Shuihudi 睡虎地秦墓竹簡整理小組, *Bamboo slips of Qin tomb of Shuihudi* 《睡虎地秦墓竹簡》, Beijing, Cultural Relics Press, 1978. p.160.

40 The organization team of bamboo slips of Qin tomb of Shuihudi 睡虎地秦墓竹簡整理小組, *Bamboo slips of Qin tomb of Shuihudi* 《睡虎地秦墓竹簡》, Beijing, Cultural Relics Press, 1978. p.160.

41 Wang Hui王輝, Try to analyze: Servants are adjudicated, for servants' the household is not adjudicated 試析"坐隸, 隸不坐戶" [J], *Journal of MudanJiang Normal University* 《牡丹江師範學院學報（哲學社會科學版）》, 2010 (1): 59-62.

names of the legislation and some without them ; furthermore, the contexts of this group of bamboo slips involved   different aspects of the society.   It was probably copied from different parts of the Laws of Qin. It was inferred that they were simplified or cut during coping; therefore, they were not easy to be understood.[42]

Many of the Statutes written in *the Miscellaneous Excerpts from Qin Statutes* were related to military affairs. They were valuable materials for the research of the military system of Qin. We could find statutes related to the appointment and removal of officers, training of army, discipline of the battlefield, supply of war service, rewards and punishments of postwar, and so on. This fitted the actual situation of Qin, for   it was in a chaotic period: domestically   reforming to build up the state strength and nationally trying to compete with other states for annexation. On the other hand, it means that understanding military affairs was an important workload for the officials. For the same reason, to the official-learn-to-be, learning this part of the law was necessary .

In *the Statutes Concerning the Appointment of Officials*《除吏律》, it said that[43] "to (recommend and) guarantee as an official a person who has been (permanently) removed from office is fined by two suits of armor. When there is a levy, they   are appointed as probationary Overseers and temporary Assistant on probation (persons with the rank of) Shang Zao (an aristocratic

42 The organization team of bamboo slips of Qin tomb of Shuihudi 睡虎地秦墓竹簡整理小組, *Bamboo slips of Qin tomb of Shuihudi*《睡虎地秦墓竹簡》, Beijing, Cultural Relics Press, 1978. p.127.

43 A.F.P. Huleswe, *Remnants of Ch'in Law: An Annotated Translation of the Ch'in Legal and Administrative Rules of the 3rd Century B.C. Discovered in Yun-meng Prefecture*, Hu-pei Province, in 1975, Leiden,   E. J. Brill Publisher, 1985. p.102.

rank) or higher; defying the Ordinances will befined two suits of armor. When an appointment to Sergeant Major and Overseer of the crossbow archers are not made following the Statutes, as well as when crossbow archers when shooting do not hit (the target), the Commandant is fined two suits of armor. When the Overseer of the crossbow archers does not hit (the target) in shooting , he is fined two suits of armor and dismissed; the Overseer guarantees him. When a coachman has been appointed for4 years and he is unable to drive, the person who taught him is fined one shield. He is dismissed and he has to do four years' statute labor and military service." As to a statute related to punishments of military affairs, disobedience of the order would be punished; failing to arch crossbow would be punished and the leader of him would be punished by joint liability, and being unable to drive as a coachman would be punished and h is teacher would also be punished by joint liability. We could tell that there was a clear teacher/student structure of riding horses and driving in the military system. If the person fails to do what he learned to do, like driving and crossbow arching, both him and the people related (teacher of the coachman or the Commandant) would be punished. Furthermore, there were more punishments for military affairs. We could tell in *the Miscellaneous Excerpts from Qin Statutes* 《秦律雜抄》, and the following statutes were related to punishments of military affairs. If someone in the military did not meet certain goals, they would be punished. If the prefectures kept conscripts and made them retainers, the prefectures would be punished; and if the county took away the supplies of the military, the prefectures and commandant would be punished.[44] If the horse did not fit

---

44 A.F.P. Huleswe, *Remnants of Ch'in Law: An Annotated Translation of the Ch'in Legal and*

for their task of running, the prefectural controller of horses would be punished; if the selected horses failed the army test, the prefecture, the assistant prefecture, and the prefectural controller of horses would all be punished.[45] If the officials with a position of assistants and clerks or higher, and he used the pack-horses privately and profited from it, he would be punished.[46] If a person wrongly received rations; the corporals or sergeants did not denounce the messmates; the prefecture, the commandant, or the sergeant major did not arrest them, they would be punished. If the soldiers sold the rations as well as the prefecture they pass through; the corporals or sergeants did not denounce the messmates; the prefectural controller of works, the assistant and clerks of the controller of works and the sergeant major in charge did not arrest them, they would be punished. If in the place where the rations were issued or in the prefectures passed through (by the recipients) commoners buy these rations, they would be punished; if the officials have been posted and they did not arrest them, the prefect and the assistant prefect would be punished; if the arms issued to conscript which were not complete or in repair, the arsenal overseer and officials would be punished.[47] If those

---

Administrative Rules of the 3rd Century B.C. Discovered in Yun-meng Prefecture, Hu-pei Province, in 1975, Leiden, E. J. Brill Publisher, 1985. pp.102-119.

45 A.F.P. Huleswe, Remnants of Ch'in Law: An Annotated Translation of the Ch'in Legal and Administrative Rules of the 3rd Century B.C. Discovered in Yun-meng Prefecture, Hu-pei Province, in 1975, Leiden, E. J. Brill Publisher, 1985. pp.102-119.

46 A.F.P. Huleswe, Remnants of Ch'in Law: An Annotated Translation of the Ch'in Legal and Administrative Rules of the 3rd Century B.C. Discovered in Yun-meng Prefecture, Hu-pei Province, in 1975, Leiden, E. J. Brill Publisher, 1985. pp.102-119.

47 A.F.P. Huleswe, Remnants of Ch'in Law: An Annotated Translation of the Ch'in Legal and Administrative Rules of the 3rd Century B.C. Discovered in Yun-meng Prefecture, Hu-pei Province, in 1975, Leiden, E. J. Brill Publisher, 1985. pp.102-119.

assigned for a levy returned and the statement was made as levy complete, then the documents showed another way, this man would be punished; if a man claimed that he was surrounded in battle and broke through and escaped, then turned out he did not arrive at the scene of the fighting, he would be punished and if the corporal and the members of his squad knew it and did not denounce it, they would be punished as well.[48] In *the Miscellaneous Excerpts from Qin Statutes*《秦律雜抄》, one situation of the military affairs would be rewarded. It was the situation that someone died in battle for the service without surrendering. Then his successor would be rewarded. However, if later it was shown that he did not die, the successor would be divested of the aristocratic rank and the men of his group should be punished (Scholar Hulsewé, A. F. P. considers the meaning of the original text was "his group of five was freed of punishment"; however, in this case, it was talking about the situation of consequence and the meaning of "除" should be punished and not be freed). And the men who had not died should return and be a bond-servant.[49] In the meanwhile, the enemies who surrender were made bond-servants as the punishment in the military affairs.[50]

There was some discussions of the meaning of the name of the

---

48 A.F.P. Huleswe, *Remnants of Ch'in Law: An Annotated Translation of the Ch'in Legal and Administrative Rules of the 3rd Century B.C. Discovered in Yun-meng Prefecture*, Hu-pei Province, in 1975, Leiden, E. J. Brill Publisher, 1985. pp.102-119.

49 A.F.P. Huleswe, *Remnants of Ch'in Law: An Annotated Translation of the Ch'in Legal and Administrative Rules of the 3rd Century B.C. Discovered in Yun-meng Prefecture*, Hu-pei Province, in 1975, Leiden, E. J. Brill Publisher, 1985. pp.102-119.

50 A.F.P. Huleswe, *Remnants of Ch'in Law: An Annotated Translation of the Ch'in Legal and Administrative Rules of the 3rd Century B.C. Discovered in Yun-meng Prefecture*, Hu-pei Province, in 1975, Leiden, E. J. Brill Publisher, 1985. pp.102-119.

regulation *theStatutes on Hardship* 《中勞律》.[51] The organization team of bamboo slips of the Qin tomb of Shuihudi explained the bamboo slip as: "Persons who venture greatly to increase the number of their years of hardship are fined one suit of armor and the hardship is canceled."[52] The explanation of the regulation was not hard to understand; however, some scholars brought up a question related to the title of this bamboo slip saying that accuracy of it could be discussed.[53] The organization team of bamboo slips of the Qin tomb of Shuihudi said that "勞"should be "the credit of hardship", but there was some ambiguity about what was "中". Some research said that "中" might have the meaning of "reached" or "justified", concerning which , it was a more appropriate interpretation of the title of this regulation. As far as the author concerned, the accurate explanation of the title of this bamboo slips needs further discussion.

For the discussion about the accuracy of the title of the bamboo slips in *the Miscellaneous Excerpts from Qin Statutes* 《秦律雜抄》, except regulation *the Statutes on Hardship* 《中勞律》, there was another one which was fully discussed. It was *the Major of Government Carriages' Statutes of Hunting*《公車司馬獵律》. In this material, the organization team of bamboo slips of the Qin tomb of Shuihudi explained the bamboo slip

---

51 A.F.P. Huleswe, *Remnants of Ch'in Law: An Annotated Translation of the Ch'in Legal and Administrative Rules of the 3rd Century B.C. Discovered in Yun-meng Prefecture*, Hu-pei Province, in 1975, Leiden, E. J. Brill Publisher, 1985. p.109.

52 A.F.P. Huleswe, *Remnants of Ch'in Law: An Annotated Translation of the Ch'in Legal and Administrative Rules of the 3rd Century B.C. Discovered in Yun-meng Prefecture*, Hu-pei Province, in 1975, Leiden, E. J. Brill Publisher, 1985, p.109.

53 Huang Liuzhu 黃留珠, Interpretation of the Statutes on Hardship of strips of Qin 秦簡《中勞律》釋義[J], *Relics and Museology*《文博》, 06/1997:65-70.

as: "For hunting tigers, two carriages from a squad. When the tiger has not yet crossed the… and they pursue him and the tiger turns back, they are fined one suit of armor. When the tiger escapes and they do not catch it, (the occupants of) the carriages are fined one suit of armor. When the tiger is about to attack, the foot-soldiers come out and shoot it; if they do not catch it, they are fined one suit of armor. When a leopard escapes and it is not caught, the fine is one shield. The Major of Government Carriages' Statutes of Hunting." The material did not contain   many arguments, but   it was the title of the bamboo slip, *the Major of Government Carriages' Statutes of Hunting*《公車司馬獵律》, which was argued by some scholars. They said that, from the perspective of philology there is a likelihood that   this title could be separated into two titles and belonged to two different regulations.[54] Other scholars[55] showed different opinions. He said that in the studies of the original bamboo slips, normally, dots were usually used to separate different sections of the contents whether   the titles were written in the front like *the Statutes Concerning the Appointment of Officials*《除吏律》,[56] or written in the middle like *theStatutes on Hardship* 《中勞律》,[57] or written in the end

---

54 Chin-yen Lin 林清源, Heading Patterns of the Qin Dynasty Bamboo Slips from Shuihudi 睡虎地秦簡標題格式析論論 [J], *Bulletin of Institute of History and Philology*《歷史語言研究所集刊》, 12/2002(73): 790-793.

55 Cao Lvning 曹旅寧, Problems of the Statute Title of the *Major of Official Carriages* of Strips of Shuihudi of Qin睡虎地秦簡《公車司馬獵律》的律名問題, *Archaeology*《考古》, 2011(5): 78-80.

56 A.F.P. Huleswe, *Remnants of Ch'in Law: An Annotated Translation of the Ch'in Legal and Administrative Rules of the 3rd Century B.C. Discovered in Yun-meng Prefecture*, Hu-pei Province, in 1975, Leiden,   E. J. Brill Publisher, 1985, p.102.

57 A.F.P. Huleswe, *Remnants of Ch'in Law: An Annotated Translation of the Ch'in Legal and Administrative Rules of the 3rd Century B.C. Discovered in Yun-meng Prefecture*, Hu-pei Province, in 1975, Leiden,   E. J. Brill Publisher, 1985, p.109.

like *theStatutes Concerning the Lobbyist* 《遊士律》.[58] And *the Major of Government Carriages' Statutes of Hunting* 《公車司馬獵律》 fitted the pattern with a dot in front of it as a separation. Furthermore, the contextual clues to the meaning of the previous bamboo slip or the following bamboo slip had clear different sections, which inferred that *the Major of Government Carriages' Statutes of Hunting* 《公車司馬獵律》 as a title belonged to one section but not two sections.

There were quite a few regulations for the official-learn-to-be to learn about military affairs in *the Miscellaneous Excerpts from Qin Statutes* 《秦律雜抄》. We could tell the proportion of the legal material of military affairs was big and it was important for both their daily life and educational life. And in this group of statutes, the one statute which was the most related to the education system of the official-learn-to-be was *the Statutes Concerning the Appointment of Retainers* 《除弟子律》.

TheStatutes Concerning the Appointment of Retainers 《除弟子律》 [59] was closely related to the education system of official-learn-to-be. The meaning of the original text was discussed by varies scholars; some said the meaning of the text was "once a student who finishes the study, and his status as a student should be dismissed;if one has graduated but his student status did not be dismissed, the official in charge of the student status should be

---

58 A.F.P. Huleswe, *Remnants of Ch'in Law: An Annotated Translation of the Ch'in Legal and Administrative Rules of the 3rd Century B.C. Discovered in Yun-meng Prefecture*, Hu-pei Province, in 1975, Leiden, E. J. Brill Publisher, 1985, p.104.

59 A.F.P. Huleswe, *Remnants of Ch'in Law: An Annotated Translation of the Ch'in Legal and Administrative Rules of the 3rd Century B.C. Discovered in Yun-meng Prefecture*, Hu-pei Province, in 1975, Leiden, E. J. Brill Publisher, 1985, p.105.

punished"[60]. However, other scholars[61][62][63] had a second opinion of the original text. The research team of the bamboo slips of Yunmeng Shuihudi and scholar Hulsewé, A. F. P. considers the meaning of the original text was "when (a person) is warranted to appoint retainers (but) the population register does not allow this, (or) when appointments are made carelessly, (such case) are all punished by shaving off the beard and being made a Hou." Even there was disagreement with the explanation of the original text; we could find in both explanations that there was registration/student status of the education system of official-learn-to-be in Qin. One thing could be pointed out in the education system of official-learn-to-be in Qin. Following the original text, it was said, "employment of one's retainers in excess (of the norms established by) the Statutes, as well as beating them, is fined one suit of armor; if the skin is broken (the fine is) two suits of armor."[64]This means that, during that time, the retainers/officials could employ and even beat the students in the range of the law.

---

60 Zhang Jinguang 張金光, *the Research of Qin's System*《秦制研究》, Shanghai, Shanghai Guji Press, 2004, p.711.

61 The organization team of bamboo slips of Qin tomb of Shuihudi 睡虎地秦墓竹簡整理小組, *Bamboo slips of Qin tomb of Shuihudi*《睡虎地秦墓竹簡》, Beijing, Cultural Relics Press, 1978.

62 A.F.P. Huleswe, *Remnants of Ch'in Law: An Annotated Translation of the Ch'in Legal and Administrative Rules of the 3rd Century B.C. Discovered in Yun-meng Prefecture*, Hu-pei Province, in 1975, Leiden, E. J. Brill Publisher, 1985.

63 Li Qintong 李勤通, Zhou Dongping 周東平, Education System of Official Carrier in the Regulations and Laws of the Initial Stage of Qin 秦漢初期律令中的史官職業教育體系[J], *Modern University Education* 《現代大學教育》, 2016(1):76-81.

64 A.F.P. Huleswe, *Remnants of Ch'in Law: An Annotated Translation of the Ch'in Legal and Administrative Rules of the 3rd Century B.C. Discovered in Yun-meng Prefecture*, Hu-pei Province, in 1975, Leiden, E. J. Brill Publisher, 1985, p.105.

In the meanwhile, there was only one group of statutes, *the Statutes Concerning the Appointment of Officials* 《除吏律》 [65] having a similar name with *the Statutes concerning the Establishment of Officials* 《置吏律》 of *the Eighteen Qin Statutes* 《秦律十八篇》. The different types of the statutes of *the Miscellaneous Experts from Qin Statutes,* such as *the Statutes Concerning the Appointment of Officials* 《除吏律》, *the Statutes Concerning the Lobbyist* 《遊士律》, [66] *the Statutes Concerning the Appointment of Retainers* 《除弟子律》, [67] *the Statutes on Hardship* 《中勞律》, [68] *theStatutes on Storage* 《臧律》, [69] *the Major of Government Carriages' Statutes of Hunting* 《公車司馬獵律》, [70] *the Statutes Concerning Rating of Cows and Sheep* 《牛羊課》, [71] *the Statutes Concerning Enrolment* 《傅

---

65 A.F.P. Huleswe, *Remnants of Ch'in Law: An Annotated Translation of the Ch'in Legal and Administrative Rules of the 3rd Century B.C. Discovered in Yun-meng Prefecture*, Hu-pei Province, in 1975, Leiden, E. J. Brill Publisher, 1985, p.102.

66 A.F.P. Huleswe, *Remnants of Ch'in Law: An Annotated Translation of the Ch'in Legal and Administrative Rules of the 3rd Century B.C. Discovered in Yun-meng Prefecture*, Hu-pei Province, in 1975, Leiden, E. J. Brill Publisher, 1985, p.104.

67 A.F.P. Huleswe, *Remnants of Ch'in Law: An Annotated Translation of the Ch'in Legal and Administrative Rules of the 3rd Century B.C. Discovered in Yun-meng Prefecture*, Hu-pei Province, in 1975, Leiden, E. J. Brill Publisher, 1985, p.105.

68 A.F.P. Huleswe, *Remnants of Ch'in Law: An Annotated Translation of the Ch'in Legal and Administrative Rules of the 3rd Century B.C. Discovered in Yun-meng Prefecture*, Hu-pei Province, in 1975, Leiden, E. J. Brill Publisher, 1985, p.109.

69 A.F.P. Huleswe, *Remnants of Ch'in Law: An Annotated Translation of the Ch'in Legal and Administrative Rules of the 3rd Century B.C. Discovered in Yun-meng Prefecture*, Hu-pei Province, in 1975, Leiden, E. J. Brill Publisher, 1985, p.110.

70 A.F.P. Huleswe, *Remnants of Ch'in Law: An Annotated Translation of the Ch'in Legal and Administrative Rules of the 3rd Century B.C. Discovered in Yun-meng Prefecture*, Hu-pei Province, in 1975, Leiden, E. J. Brill Publisher, 1985, p.113.

71 A.F.P. Huleswe, *Remnants of Ch'in Law: An Annotated Translation of the Ch'in Legal and Administrative Rules of the 3rd Century B.C. Discovered in Yun-meng Prefecture*, Hu-pei Province, in 1975, Leiden, E. J. Brill Publisher, 1985, p.115.

律》，[72] *the Statutes Concerning Border Defense*《敦表律》，[73] *the Statutes Concerning the Arrest if Robbers*《捕盜律》，[74] *the Statutes Concerning Military Service*《戍律》，[75] were representing the complexity and variety of the legal system of Qin, and evermore, it proved again that, *the Bamboo slips of Qin tomb of Shuihudi* could only represent a part of the legal teaching/learning materials of the education system of official-learn-to-be of Qin.

4.4. *The Models for Sealing and Investigating* 《封診式》

There were 98 bamboo slips of *the Models for Sealing and Investigating* 《封診式》 and were placed on the right side of the head of the tomb owner Xi with *the Chronological Record and the daily book*《日書》. According to the organization team of bamboo slips of Qin tomb of Shuihudi, both *the Models for Sealing and Investigating*《封診式》 and *the Chronological Record and the daily book*《日書》 were lying scattered as in long overstock and reorganized by the organization team of bamboo slips of Qin tomb of Shuihudi. The order of the content was based on the main content of the

---

72 A.F.P. Huleswe, *Remnants of Ch'in Law: An Annotated Translation of the Ch'in Legal and Administrative Rules of the 3rd Century B.C. Discovered in Yun-meng Prefecture*, Hu-pei Province, in 1975, Leiden, E. J. Brill Publisher, 1985, p.115.

73 A.F.P. Huleswe, *Remnants of Ch'in Law: An Annotated Translation of the Ch'in Legal and Administrative Rules of the 3rd Century B.C. Discovered in Yun-meng Prefecture*, Hu-pei Province, in 1975, Leiden, E. J. Brill Publisher, 1985, p.117.

74 A.F.P. Huleswe, *Remnants of Ch'in Law: An Annotated Translation of the Ch'in Legal and Administrative Rules of the 3rd Century B.C. Discovered in Yun-meng Prefecture*, Hu-pei Province, in 1975, Leiden, E. J. Brill Publisher, 1985, p.118.

75 A.F.P. Huleswe, *Remnants of Ch'in Law: An Annotated Translation of the Ch'in Legal and Administrative Rules of the 3rd Century B.C. Discovered in Yun-meng Prefecture*, Hu-pei Province, in 1975, Leiden, E. J. Brill Publisher, 1985, p.118.

bamboo slip, taking the unearthed position of the bamboo slips into consideration.[76]

As we all known, the materials of the newly excavated documents were always lying scattered. And a group of materials of which each section had a title was not very common. Even more, in the perspective of legal learning materials for the officials-learn-to-be, *the Models for Sealing and Investigating* 《封診式》 was actually a group of summarized case law for them to study. As a matter of fact, within this group of legal learning/teaching materials of Qin state, some scholars pointed out that "式" of "封診式" ("model" of "*the Models for sealing and Investigating*") had two meanings: official documents and judicial process. *The Models for Sealing and Investigating* 《封診式》 was the earliest "model/式" we have seen from Bamboo slips of Qin tomb of Shuihudi, which was years earlier than "*The Models of Datong*" (大統式) from the period of Wei-Jin (魏晉時期).[77]

There was something missing from other groups of bamboo slips. There were 25 sections of the *Models for Sealing and Investigating* 《封診式》 ; each section had its title on the first bamboo slip and most of them were with a format beginning of "report 爰書". There was a certain format to write down all the regulation in *the Models for Sealing and Investigating* 《封診式》 . Because the tips of some strip were broken off, the titles of two of the sections were missing. The other 23 had the title of each section.[78]

---

76 The organization team of bamboo slips of Qin tomb of Shuihudi 睡虎地秦墓竹簡整理小組, *Bamboo slips of Qin tomb of Shuihudi*《睡虎地秦墓竹簡》, Beijing, Cultural Relics Press, 1978. p.244.

77 Zhang Xiaolei 張孝蕾, The Study of Sealed Postmortem Shi 睡虎地秦簡《封診式》研究 [D], Changsha, Hunan University, 05/2013.

78 A.F.P. Huleswe, *Remnants of Ch'in Law: An Annotated Translation of the Ch'in Legal and*

They were: *Trying lawsuits* 治獄, *Interrogating* 訊獄, *Under interrogation* 有鞫, *Sealing and Guarding* 封守, *Re-interrogation* 覆, *A robber voluntarily denounces himself* 盜自告, *Arrest* □捕, *Stealing a horse* 盜馬, *A dispute about a cow* 爭牛, *Gang robbery* 群盜, *Snatching a head away* 奪首, *Denouncing a slave* 告臣, *Tattooing a female slave* 黥妾, *Banishing a son* 遷子, Denouncing a son 告子, Leprosy 癘, Death by murderous intent 賊死, Death by hanging 經死, Robbery by tunneling 穴盜, A miscarriage 出子, Poisonous words 毒言, Fornication 奸, An absconder comes forward voluntarily 亡自出.

Sections of *Trying lawsuits* 治獄 and *Interrogating* 訊獄 should be the first two sections of *the Models for Sealing and Investigating* 《封診式》 based on its location of the document. These two were the procedural law for the officials to judge the   cases. There was the regulation of case hearing and case questioning, functioning as complementary law. The rest of twenty-three sections were documental patterns based on cases. The documental pattern had two functions; one was as the pattern for various documents writing for officers in Qin; the other was as a reference for case hearing.[79]

Depending on different situations, as procedural law, these two regulations emphasized the importance of the best case which has a true statement instead of using bastinado.[80] However, if necessary, it could use

---

Administrative Rules of the 3rd Century B.C. Discovered in Yun-meng Prefecture, Hu-pei Province, in 1975, Leiden, E. J. Brill Publisher, 1985, pp.183-207.

79 Zhang Xiaolei 張孝蕾, The Study of Sealed Postmortem Shi 睡虎地秦簡《封診式》研究 [D], Changsha, Hunan University, 05/2013.

80 A.F.P. Huleswe, *Remnants of Ch'in Law: An Annotated Translation of the Ch'in Legal and Administrative Rules of the 3rd Century B.C. Discovered in Yun-meng Prefecture*, Hu-pei Province, in 1975, Leiden, E. J. Brill Publisher, 1985, p.184.

torture to coerce a statement and noted down the bastinado during interrogation.[81] We could see the wisdom of the official who made this regulation about the procedure of interrogation saying: "If in trying lawsuits it is possible employing documents to track down his words, obtaining the facts of the person without using this bastinado is the best; applying the bastinado id interior, (for) when there is fear, (everything) is spoiled."[82] If we put this regulation in the present days, it still fits in our society; in other words, the value of it was a wise outcome of the accumulation of the wisdom of the people in ancient times.   And the details of interrogation were listed in *Interrogating* 訊獄, saying that, "In all cases of interrogating in a lawsuit one should first listen fully to the words and note these down, each (of the persons questioned) set out his statement. Although (the investigator) knows that he is lying, there is no need to insist every time. When his statement has been completely noted down, but is not understandable, then insist on the points necessary. When having insisted, one has again fully listened and noted down the explanatory statements, one looks again at other unexplained points and insists again on these. When one has insisted to the limit, but he has repeatedly lied, changing his statement   and not submitting, then, for those people whom the Statutes warrant to be bastinadoed, bastinado them. When bastinadoing him, be sure to note down: Report – Because X repeatedly changed his words and made no explanatory statement, X has been

---

81 A.F.P. Huleswe, *Remnants of Ch'in Law: An Annotated Translation of the Ch'in Legal and Administrative Rules of the 3rd Century B.C. Discovered in Yun-meng Prefecture*, Hu-pei Province, in 1975, Leiden, E. J. Brill Publisher, 1985, pp.185-186.

82 A.F.P. Huleswe, *Remnants of Ch'in Law: An Annotated Translation of the Ch'in Legal and Administrative Rules of the 3rd Century B.C. Discovered in Yun-meng Prefecture*, Hu-pei Province, in 1975, Leiden, E. J. Brill Publisher, 1985, p.183.

interrogated with the bastinado."[83] With this document, we could see that the level of making procedural law was not low, it separated different responses to different cases while interrogating, and logically, they all fitted in the reality during the period of Qin.

Except for these two sections, other sections were documents which covered wild range perspectives of the society and most of them were written as case law. *The Models for Sealing and Investigating* 《封診式》 involved different kinds of cases, different official documents summarized as a format using case investigations, case interrogations, and case procuration.

Some sections of — *The Models for Sealing and Investigating*《封診式》 focused on the judicial process, such as case questioning process, attachment process, inspection process, suing process, and case hearing process. The first four processes specifically regulate the last process.[84]

A/甲, B/乙, C/丙, D/丁 always represented the people of the cases and this format was believed to make other people read and understand the case easier. However, the pattern using A, B, C, D of *the Models for Sealing and Investigating* 《封診式》 was different from *the Answers to Questions Concerning Qin Statutes*《法律答問》. In the cases of *the Answers to Questions Concerning Qin Statutes*《法律答問》, the people involved in the case was represented by the order of A/甲, B/乙, C/丙, D/丁. However,

---

83 A.F.P. Huleswe, *Remnants of Ch'in Law: An Annotated Translation of the Ch'in Legal and Administrative Rules of the 3rd Century B.C. Discovered in Yun-meng Prefecture*, Hu-pei Province, in 1975, Leiden, E. J. Brill Publisher, 1985, p.184.

84 Zhang Xiaolei 張孝蕾, The Study of Sealed Postmortem Shi 睡虎地秦簡《封診式》研究 [D], Changsha, Hunan University, 05/2013.

in *the Models for Sealing and Investigating*《封診式》, the order was not always A/甲, B/乙, C/丙, D/丁. "B/乙" was always not showing in the case. Some scholars believed that it represented a special usage of "B/乙". The writer of *the Models for Sealing and Investigating*《封診式》 might probably avoid "B/乙" and use "A/甲", "C/丙". In the meanwhile, the writer of *the Models for Sealing and Investigating*《封診式》 might intend to not to use "B/乙" to represent the criminals. And this special pattern could be a legal term in the legislative procedure of Qin.[85] This format was also an extinguished pattern for the organization team of bamboo slips of Qin tomb of Shuihudi to better organize *the Models for Sealing and Investigating*《封診式》.

These cases involved in *the Models for Sealing and Investigating*《封診式》 could reflect that chaotic situation of the Qin state during the transformation of society. To those case-related criminal laws, lots of contents were pointed to theft, robbery, and murder. The writer could somehow summarize the case as references for others to learn, which meant that those crimes were not rare, and the society needed legal regulation for them to understand the consequence of those crimes. In the meanwhile, *the Models for Sealing and Investigating*《封診式》, as the learning/teaching materials for officials-learn-to-be to study and for officials to try cases as consultation, we could tell it is very similar with our Case Law nowadays.

The legal teaching materials of Legalist's school almost cover every aspect of the society, and in the above analysis, the forms of the regulations in

---

85 Zhao Chao 趙超, An Investigation and Analysis of the Anonymous Pronoun "Yi"in "Feng Zhen Shi"《封診式》中隱名代詞"乙"的考察分析, *Journal of Chongqing University of Arts and Sciences*《重慶文理學院學報》[J], 03/2017, 36(2):57-63.

pre-Han China　had the simple one such as statute law on the one hand, but on the other hand case law was also well known by the officials and people. It is a surprising outcome for the researcher to discover　the abundant and rich details of the legal teaching materials of pre-Han China.

Chapter Five
The teaching material of Literacy 文字教材

5.1. Introduction of the teaching material of literacy of Pre-Han China

Except for learning legal materials, officials-learn-to-be have to learn enough Chinese characters and after achieving a certain amount of the words they have to   deal with their working life.   In this chapter, the author   will write about the literacy materials that the officials-learn-to-be had to learn. And I will conduct a further analysis of the social and structural reasons which shaped   the education of officials in the literacy way.

As we all know, if we want to deal with our daily issues, learning how to read is the basic skill for people to pick up. There was no difference with the people in Qin China. Lots of people nowadays consider that the literacy rate during Qin China was low or even simply think the people of Qin China were illiterate. Via   the handed documents, we find the case is not like how we take for granted, and the newly excavated documents help us further prove the fact is that the people of Pre-Han China were quite acknowledged and some of them could read and write. During the Han dynasty, the education system was built more scientifically and the structure of the education system was refined. The education of plebeians, general officers, and sovereigns were all refined during the period of Qin China. Base on the unification of Qin Emperor Yingzheng, the vocabulary was once unified; and since the society was developing, and the quantities of vocabulary have been increased.

However, after the unification of Qin Emperor Yingzheng gave an order to burn books , especially   the Confucian classics, so we doubt   the quantities of the vocabulary may be decreased rather than be increased.

Different social classes had different needs for the quantity of vocabulary. Logically, we can easily have a summary of the quantity of vocabulary for different social classes in Qin.

i As for the plebeians, due to the nature of their workload and daily life, they may probably have a limited vocabulary or even could not read a single word.

ii As for   officers, based on the education policies of Qin (law as education 以法為教 and officials as teachers 以吏為師), it was not hard to have an assumption that, the officers had to at least reach the level to understand all the characters of the laws, and know intimately the meaning of the regulation so that they could educate other people about the meaning of the law.

iii The sovereign, standing on the top of the social class, had a responsibility to make policies   for running the state, so being highly educated and having a big amount of vocabulary were inevitable, whether   he was an accomplished ruler or a fatuous ruler.

Understanding the content of the teaching material of literacy of Qin China   not only facilitated   the exploration of the education system in ancient times but also did   good to the comprehension of the development of Chinese culture.

5.2. The handed documents of the teaching material of literacy during Pre-Qin China

In the main discussion of this chapter, we point out that both inscriptions and wordbooks play valuable roles for us to understand the situation of the teaching materials of literacy in Pre-Qin China.

In the handed-down documents, we can find different discretion about people learning literacy in the educational system. In the various aspects of the society, the Han dynasty carried on the system of Qin dynasty 漢承秦制, so, following the documents found related to the Han dynasty, we may sort out the refine content of the characters they learn of Qin China and forwardly, find the more accurate details of the teaching materials of literacy.

5.2.1. The Chinese paleography and development of the teaching material of literacy of QinChina

If we want to find out the teaching material of the literacy of Qin China, understanding the Chinese paleography may give us a more complete picture of the concept. The Chinese paleography is a well-researched academic area. Quantities of scholars pay attention to this interesting topic in the academic field of using the perspectives among archaeology, history, sociology, philology, and pedagogy. Thanks would be paid to those senior scholars[1][2][3][4]

---

1   Edward L. Shaughnessy, *New Sources of Early Chinese History: An Introduction to the Reading of Inscriptions and Manuscripts*, Univ of California Inst of East, 11/1997.

2   Qiu Xigui 裘錫圭, *Essentials of Philology*《文字學概要》, Beijing, The Commercial Press, 07/2001.

3   Tang Lan 唐蘭, *Introduction of Paleography*《古文字學導論》, Jina, Shangdong Qilu Press, 01/1981.

who made a profound effort and did valuable research about the inscriptions and manuscripts of Early Chinese History and philology of early China.

The Chinese paleography is a historical and analytical study concerned with ancient characters and writings. According to the authoritative scholar Chen Mengjia 陳夢家, two types of materials are fundamental to studies in Chinese paleography,. Generally speaking, they were categorized including the inscribed oracle bones and the inscription on the bronzes and other antiquities and the dictionaries, the rhyme books, and other works. The first type includes the inscribed oracle bones and the inscription on the bronzes and other antiquities, from the Shang 商 to the Han 漢 dynasty. The second type includes the dictionaries, the rhyme books, and other works from the pre-Han to the present.[5] Both types can provide a great amount of information to us. It was considered that the first type of material is more important because it contains the original texts of monuments of that time.[6] In this case, it was the materials that we could find in the newly excavated documents. The importance of the second type lies mainly in that it links the ancient and the modern characters together and it could be referred to as the handed-down documents. However, the errors in various recopying and reprinting books have made textual criticism a necessary adjunct to this type. This kind of false-left situation was not easy to avoid and almost inevitable. That is the reason we should pay extra attention to the usage of those handed-

---

4 Hu Pu'an 胡樸安, *Elementary Knowledge of Philology*《文字學常識》, Beijing, Zhonghua Book Company, 01/2010.

5 Chen Mengjia 陳夢家, *An Introduction to Chinese Paleography*《中國文字學》, Beijing, Zhonghua Book Company, 2006. p.261.

6 Chen Mengjia 陳夢家, *An Introduction to Chinese Paleography*《中國文字學》, Beijing, Zhonghua Book Company, 2006.

down documents and the newly excavated documents havetheir advantages. In recent years the study of Chinese paleography has become one of the most important courses of Chinese offered in universities in China. And Chinese paleography is closely related to the teaching materials of literacy. The department of Chinese is divided into two sections: one in Chinese literature and the other in Chinese paleography and philology. Scholar Chen Mengjia researched the work in paleography which   was delivered as follows:[7]

  (1)   Introduction to Chinese Paleography

    (a) Pre-Han

    (b) Post-Han

  (2)   Research in Chinese paleography

    (a) Inscriptions

    (b) Wordbooks

  (3)   History of paleography

The Han dynasty basically carried forward accede from Qin empire, and in *the Statutes of Commandant*《尉律》of Han dynasty, which quoted by Xu Shen 許慎 in the preface of his book *First Chinese Dictionary* (Shuo Wen Jie Zi)《說文解字·敘》, it said that to be an official of paperwork/document, there were standards to meet: one was to be at least 17 years old, the other was to become literate of 9000 characters.[8] As we discussed in the previous chapters, we know that if people wanted to be an official in Qin dynasty, they had to learn enough words to tackle the problem which happened in their position, so in this chapter; we are going to talk about the teaching material of

---

7   Chen Mengjia 陳夢家, *An Introduction to Chinese Paleography*《中國文字學》, Beijing, Zhonghua Book Company, 2006. p.262.

8   《說文解字·敘》:"學童十七已上 ,始試 ,諷籀書九千字 ,乃得為吏。"

literacy using the newly excavated documents.

5.2.2. The handed-down documents related to the teaching material of literacy during Pre-Han China

In the book of *the Han Shu,* Ban Gu wrote about the school ages and content: the child at the age of 8 starts school (Xiao Xue 小學), learning Liu Jia 六甲,[9] Wu Fang 五方,[10] characters, and counting.[11]In *the Chapter of Bao Fu* of *Da Dai Li Ji/the book of Rites of Dai De*《大戴禮記·保傅篇》 it said that: when the ancient people are 8 years old, they go and live outside, learn Xiao Yi 小藝, perform Xiao Jie 小節; (when they are old enough) to tie up hair then they study Da Xue 大學, learn Da Yi 大藝, learn Da Jie 大節. In *the Chapter of Nei Ze* of *Xiao Dai Li Ji/the book of Rites of Dai Sheng*《小戴禮記·內則篇》 it said that: (When people are) 6 years old teach them Math and direction,: (When people are) 9 years old teach them the first and the fifteenth day of the lunar month and count days using Heavenly Stems and Earthly Branches, (When people are) 10 years old, they go out and learn from teachers, live outside, learn writing and math. Compared with Da Xue 大學, the ancients called literacy Xiao Xue 小學. Through these documents, they justified the basic education system concluding Xiao Xue and Da Xue was transferred from all in a muddle to an organized structure

---

9 In ancient China, people counted days using Heavenly Stems 天干 and Earthly Branches 地支, there were 6六甲of them：Jia Zi甲子, Jia Xu 甲戌, Jia Shen 甲申, Jia Wu 甲午, Jia Chen 甲辰, Jia Yin 甲寅.

10 In ancient China, people used Wu Fang 五方(meaning east, south, west, north and middle) to tell directions of geography.

11 〔Han〕Ban Gu〔漢〕班固, *Han Shu/History of the Former Han*《漢書》, Shanghai, Shanghai Guji Press, 12/2003, p744.

with teaching objects and materials during the Qin and Han dynasties.

Some scholars summarized that child education was getting into a systematic phase with teaching materials and type of organization after the Qin and Han dynasties.[12] Some scholars considered the improvement of education during that time was one of the outstanding cultural achievements, and child education during that time was worth paying special attention through the ancient education history of China.[13]   And from the perspective of family education, some scholars thought that the Qin and Han dynasties were a period shaping the frame of family education; all the development and perfection of family education was based on this frame.[14]

Furthermore, due to *the Han Shu,* there were many documents related to the wordbook as the teaching material of literacy and the content of Xiao Xue was varied.[15]   There were a total of 45 different chapters of literacy for Xiao Xue students to learn. These kinds of wordbooks were all written crossing the time zone from Zhou dynasty 周朝 to Eastern Han Dynasty 東漢. Within this handed-down documents, 3 wordbooks of Pre-Qin China are documented, namely   the Book of Shi Zhou《史籀》, with 15 chapters and with remarks   by Ban Gu saying the ruler of Zhou dynasty Xuan 周宣王 ordered the court historian 太史 to write 15 chapters of Da Zuan 大篆,

---

12 Qiao Weiping 喬衛平, Cheng Peijie 程培傑,*Child Education of Ancient Chian*《中國古代幼兒教育》,Hefei, Anhui Educational Publishing House 安徽教育出版社,07/1989,p.153.

13 Wang Zijin 王子今,*Child Life of Han Dynasty*《漢代兒童生活》,Xi'an, San Qin Chu Ban She 三秦出版社,09/2012,pp.90-111.

14 Ma Yong 馬鏞,*Educational History of Chinese Families*《中國家庭教育史》,Changsha, Hunan Education Publishing House 湖南教育出版社,05/1997,pp.43-44.

15 〔Han〕Ban Gu〔漢〕班固, *Han Shu/History of the Former Han*《漢書》, Shanghai, Shanghai Guji Press, 12/2003, p1187.

among which 9 chapters remained at the time of Jian Wu (25 A.D. to 56 A.D.); the Book of Ba Ti Liu Ji《八體六技》; the Book of Cang Jie《倉頡》, with the combination of 7 chapters of Cang Jie《倉頡》written by chancellor Li Si 李斯 of Qin, 6 chapters of the Book Yuan Li《爰歷》 written by an officer of carriage 中車府令 Zhao Gao 趙高 and 7 chapters of Bo Xue《博學》,written by court historian 太史 Hu Wujin 胡毋敬.

The following table may give us detailed information on the existing information of Pre-Han and Han from the handed-down documents of the paleography:

Time	Author	Book	Remark
During the Emperor Xuan in Western Zhou Dynasty 周宣王時期	Shi Liu 史留（籀）	15 chapter of The Shi Zhou《史籀》15 章	This book is the main part of the wordbooks of The Cang Jie《倉頡》, The Yuan Li《爰歷》and The Bo Xue《博學》
Qin	Li Si 李斯	7 chapter of The Cang Jie《倉頡》7 章	After the unification of the Qin dynasty, the books of the introduction of characters still used the written font of Xiao Zuan 小篆. During Han dynasty, these three (the Cang Jie《倉頡》, the Yuan Li《爰歷》and the Bo Xue《博學》) were combined into a book and called the Cang Jie《倉頡》., With a total number of 3300 Chinese characters, the Cang Jie《倉頡》included 55 chapters and 60
Qin	Zhao Gao 趙高	6 chapters of The Yuan Li《爰歷》6 章	
Qin	Hu Wujin 胡毋敬	7 chapters of The Bo Xue《博學》7 章	

Time	Author	Book	Remark
			characters were grouped into 1 chapter.
During Emperor Wu in Western Han Dynasty 漢武帝時	Sima Xiangru 司馬相如	*The chapter of Fan Jiang*《凡將篇》	
During Emperor Yuan in Western Han Dynasty 漢元帝時	Shi You 史遊	*The chapter of Ji Jiu*《急就篇》	
During Emperor Cheng in Western Han Dynasty 漢成帝時	Li Chang 李長	*The chapter of Yuan Shang*《元尚篇》	
During Emperor Ping in Western Han Dynasty 漢平帝時	Yang Xiong 揚雄	*The chapter of Xu Zuan*《訓篆篇》	These three books were combined into the book called *the San Cang*《三倉》. It used the written font of Li calligraphy 隸書 and the written font of Xiao Zuan 小篆 and Da Zuan 大篆字體 were abandoned. In the meanwhile, for the easy memory and catchy reading aloud for children, *the San Cang*《三倉》 was written with four characters in line and rhyme. For the structure of *the San Cang*《三倉》, it was separated into three volumes,
Eastern Han Dynasty 東漢	Xu Shen 許慎	*Shuo Wen Jie Zi*《說文解字》	
Eastern Han Dynasty 東漢	Jia Fang 賈魴	*Pang Xi*《滂喜》	

Time	Author	Book	Remark
			Shuo Wen Jie Zi《說文解字》 was the first volume, and *the chapter of Xu Zuan* 《訓篡篇》 and *the Pang Xi*《滂喜》 were the second and third volumes.

5.3. The newly excavated documents of the teaching material of literacy during early-Han China

There are some newly excavated documents related to teaching materials of literacy, which were earthed for so long a time and discovered recently, and made a great impact on the research of the teaching materials of literacy. Two of them play the most important parts, including *the History Law of the Two Year Law*《二年律令·史令》 of *the Han Bamboo Slips of Zhang Jia Shan*《張家山漢簡》 and *the Chapter of Cang Jie*《倉頡篇》 *of the Han Bamboo Slips of Beijing University*《北大藏漢簡》.

5.3.1. The Two Year Law of the Han Bamboo Slips of Zhang Jia Shan 《張家山漢簡・二年律令》

The Han Bamboo Slips of Zhang Jia Shan《張家山漢簡》, which was unearthed during 1983-1984 at Jiangling 江陵 of Hubei 湖北 province, China. The newly excavated documents of *The Han Bamboo Slips of Zhang Jia Shan* was a group of bamboo strips containing 1236 bamboo strips (not including the broken strips). The content of ancient codes and records are closely related to Qin and Han dynasty. *The Han Bamboo Slips of Zhang Jia Shan*《張家山漢簡》 has high academic value and the bamboo strips were written with 8 groups of materials including legislation, military, calendar, medicine, science, and so on.[16]

There are 27 kinds of regulations　written in *theHan Bamboo Slips of Zhang Jia Shan* 《張家山漢簡》,[17] and some of them are related to the teaching material of literacy and the education system during that time. It is *the History Law of the Two Year Law*《二年律令·史令》of *the Han Bamboo Slips of Zhang Jia Shan* 《張家山漢簡》. We think　the Han dynasty carried on the system of Qin dynasty 漢承秦制, and even the *History Law of the Two Year Law* of *the Han Bamboo Slips of Zhang Jia Shan* is a newly excavated documents of Han dynasty instead of the time of Qin or Pre-Qin, and we still consider it would be helpful to our research about the teaching material of literacy.

There is a regulation of *the History Law of the Two-Year Law* of *the Han Bamboo Slips of Zhang Jia Shan* related to the education system, it said :

During that time, there were different statuses of the students called: Shi 史, Bu 卜, Zhu 祝. And the learning period of the Shi 史, Bu 卜, Zhu 祝 was three years. When students finished the stage of Shi 史, Bu 卜, Zhu 祝, they were going to start the academic stages of Da Shi 大史, Da Bu 大蔔, Da Zhu 大祝. And the schoolchild of Jun Shi 郡史 would have a unified examination in August. When the schoolchild could write 15 chapters of The Shi Liu with 5000 characters, they could get an official position as a clerk.

---

16 The Organization team of No.247 Tomb of Zhangjiashan 張家山二四七號漢墓之整理小組,*Bamboo Slips of No.247 Tomb of Zhangjiashan*《張家山漢墓竹簡[二四七號墓]》, Beijing,Cultural Relics Press, 2006.

17 The Organization team of No.247 Tomb of Zhangjiashan 張家山二四七號漢墓之整理小組,*Bamboo Slips of No.247 Tomb of Zhangjiashan*《張家山漢墓竹簡[二四七號墓]》, Beijing,Cultural Relics Press, 2006.

The schoolchild who can get the best at the examination of the Bi Ti 八體課 could be the county magistrate 縣令史.[18]

Through the newly excavated documents of *the History Law of the Two Year* Law of the Han *Bamboo Slips of Zhang Jia Shan,* we could confirm that in the education system, learning the teaching material of literacy was a requirement if one wants to be an official,. In this way he could reach the requirement of the clerk or county magistrate. Some scholars argue that the system stratification of Shi 史, Bu 卜, Zhu 祝 was a unique talent training system;[19] however, the author considers since the Han dynasty carried on the system of the Qin dynasty, this kind of education system might be built up long before Han dynasty.

5.3.2. The chapter of Cang Jie of the Han Bamboo Slips of Beijing University 《北大藏漢簡 · 倉頡篇》

Unlike the normal bamboo slips being unearthed during the discovery of tombs in China, *The Qin Bamboo Slips of Beijing University* was donated to Beijing University from overseas in 2009. After the work of cleaning, measuring, organizing and photographing by both experts from Beijing University and Changsha Bamboo Slips Museum, all the bamboo slips of this group were sorted out with a total number of 3346.[20] The scholar, after

---

18 Zhu Honglin 朱紅林, *The Explanation Collection on the Two Year Laws of Zhangjiashan Bamboo Slips* 《張家山漢簡〈二年律令〉》集釋, Beijing, Social Sciences Academic Press (China), 2005. p.280.

19 Wang Zijin 王子今, *Child Life of Han Dynasty* 《漢代兒童生活》,Xi'an, San Qin Chu Ban She 三秦出版社,09/2012,p.104.

20 The Peking University Excavated Manuscript Research Center edited北京大學出土文獻研究所編, *Peking University Bamboo Strips of Xi Han* 《北京大學藏西漢竹書》, Shanghai, Shanghai Guji Press, 09/2015, p.1.

considering comprehensive multiple factors, comparing it with the handed-down documents[21]assumed that the owner of this group of Qin bamboo slips should be an aristocrat of the Han dynasty.[22]

When we go through this newly excavated document, we find that the information of the Qin Bamboo Slips of Beijing University covers all 6 files 六略 including Liu Yi 六藝, Zhu Zi 諸子, Shi Fu 詩賦, Bing Shu 兵書, Shu Shu 數術, and Fang Ji 方技[23] mentioned in *the Han Shu*. It includes a wordbook *of the chapter of Cang Jie*《倉頡篇》, which contains the greatest amount number of characters compared with all the exiting wordbooks of Qin and Han dynasty. *The chapter of Cang Jie* of the Han Bamboo Slips of Beijing University has 53 complete bamboo slips and 34 incomplete bamboo slips. After being put together by the experts, 63 bamboo slips were completed and 18 remained missing or uncompleted.[24]

According to the aforementioned discussion, *the Cang Jie* was one of the teaching materials of literacy during Pre-Han, and the Han dynasty mostly carried on the system of Qin dynasty 漢承秦制. *The chapter of Cang Jie* of the Han bamboo slip of Beijing University may help us deeply understand what characters people of Pre-Han learn and what the teaching materials of

---

21 Liang Jing 梁靜,*Study of the unearthed Cangjie*《出土〈倉頡篇〉研究》, Beijing, Science Press,10/2015.

22 The Peking University Excavated Manuscript Research Center edited北京大學出土文獻研究所編, *Peking University Bamboo Strips of Xi Han*《北京大學藏西漢竹書》, Shanghai,Shanghai Guji Press,09/2015, pp.1-2.

23 〔Han〕Ban Gu〔漢〕班固, *Han Shu/History of the Former Han*《漢書》, Shanghai, Shanghai Guji Press, 12/2003, pp1174-1227.

24 The Peking University Excavated Manuscript Research Center edited北京大學出土文獻研究所編, *Peking University Bamboo Strips of Xi Han*《北京大學藏西漢竹書》, Shanghai,Shanghai Guji Press,09/2015,p.67.

literacy during Pre-Han were. The number of the rime categories 韻部 (including the repeated topic characters) and the chapters of the rime categories (known by the rime categories) of *the chapter of Cang Jie* of the Han bamboo slip of Beijing University were as follows:

The Rime Category	The Number of the Rime Category	Remark
Zhi 之 and Zhi 職	212	The chapter of "X Lu"「X 祿」and "Han Jian"「漢兼」belong to this rime category
Zhi 之	42	The chapter of "Kuo Cuo"「闊錯」belong to this rime category
You 幽 and Xiao 宵	39	
You 幽	130	
Yu 魚	257	The chapter of "Bi Bo"「幣帛」and "X Kui"「X 悝」belong to this rime category
Zhi 支 and Zhi 脂	20	
Zhi 支	82	The chapter of "（上齊下貝）Gou"「（上齊下貝）購」belong to this rime category
Zhi 脂	24	
Yang 陽	377	The chapter of "Zhuan Xu"「顓頊」, "Shi Yu"「室宇」, "Yun Yu"「雲雨」and "X Lun"「X 輪」belong to this rime category
Geng 耕	130	The chapter of "He Bao"「鶡鴇」belong to this rime category
Unknown	24	

Fig 5.1.[25]

---

25 The Peking University Excavated Manuscript Research Center edited北京大學出土文獻研究所編, *Peking University Bamboo Strips of Xi Han*《北京大學藏西漢竹書》, Shanghai, Shanghai Guji Press,2015.

With the total number of characters around 1300, the word count of each chapter within *the chapter of Cang Jie ofthe Han bamboo slip of Beijing University* was presumably more than 100 and most of the characters are not the same.[26]

As an important teaching material of literacy during the Qin and Han dynasty, *the chapter of Cang Jie* was not only a wordbook for the younger children to learn but also reflected the perspective of the upper class and attracted the attention of the knowledgeable people . This discovery of *the chapter of Cang Jie* helps us to clarify the original context of the famous but long-lostwordbook. In this part, we tried to sort out the original context of *the chapter of Cang Jie of the Han bamboo slip of Beijing University*, so that we could further understand what literacy the people of Qin dynasty learn during that time.

In the ancient wordbooks, to help the student to pick up words more easily , the wordbooks were usually written in a fixed pattern with a cohesive rhyme.   So, the writer/writers of the wordbook might normally categorize the rime characters and the context of the wordbook might express some pieces of opinion suited in the social value during that time. Most of the scholars consider this point of view in line   with *the chapter of Cang Jie* , saying it ought to be catchy. [2728] Scholar Hu Pingsheng even considered that

---

26 The Peking University Excavated Manuscript Research Center edited北京大學出土文獻研究所編, *Peking University Bamboo Strips of Xi Han*《北京大學藏西漢竹書》, Shanghai,Shanghai Guji Press,2015,p.67.

27 Wang Ning 王寧, Reading Han Scripts of Peking University of *Cang* 北大漢簡《蒼頡篇》讀劄（上）, The research center of the newly excavated document of Fudan 復旦大學出土文獻與古文字研究中心, 22/02/2016, http://www.gwz.fudan.edu.cn/Web/Show/2744

28 Hu Pingsheng胡平生, After Reading *Cang* 1 讀《蒼》劄記一, The research center of the

if we make the annotation of *the chapter of Cang Jie* in a not catchy way and cannot make the annotation be read through in the full text, there   might be some mistakes in understanding the meaning of the original writer.[29] We believe this assumption was correct and it can reveal some actual parts of the teaching materials of the literacy through this newly excavated document. The newly excavated document of *the chapter of Cang Jie of the Han bamboo slip of Beijing University* was no exceptional case, and it shows us the pattern of traditional wordbooks in a clear way. 4 characters are lined in one sentence as a fixed pattern to write the whole book, with the last character in one same rime category in each chapter.   All the characters within *the chapter of Cang Jieof the Han bamboo slip of Beijing University* mentioned in the following context were taken as the words the people of pre-Han and Han dynasty learn in the teaching material of literacy.

For example:

The first chapter "X Lu"「X 祿」of the chapter of Cang Jie:

"X Lu"「X 祿」

寬惠善志。桀紂迷惑，宗幽不識。冣□隸宜，□□獲得。（Strips 1）

賓劓向尚，馮奕青北。係孫褒俗，狠鷥吉忌。瘀□癱痤，（Strips 2）

疢痛遬欬。毒藥醫工，抑按啟久。嬰但捃援，何竭負戴。（Strips 3）

綌縠阪險，丘陵故舊。長緩肆延，渙奐若思。勇猛剛毅，（Strips 4）

便走巧巫。景桓昭穆，豐盈爨□。嬛替焗黑，□姆款餌。（Strips 5）

---

newly excavated document of Fudan復旦大學出土文獻與古文字研究中心, 21/12/2015, http://www.gwz.fudan.edu.cn/Web/Show/2687

29 Hu Pingsheng胡平生, After   Reading *Cang* 1 讀《蒼》劄記一,   The research   center of the newly excavated document of Fudan復旦大學出土文獻與古文字研究中心, 21/12/2015, http://www.gwz.fudan.edu.cn/Web/Show/2687

戲叢書插，顛□重該。悉起臣僕，發傳約載。趣邍觀望，（Strips 6）

行步駕服。逋逃隱匿，往來昕睞。　百五十二　　（Strips 7）

"Han Jian"「漢兼」

漢兼天下，海內並廁。胡無噍類，菹醢離異。戎翟給賽，（Strips 8）

百越貢織。餝端 XX，變大制裁。男女番殖，六畜逐字。（Strips 9）

顚 X 觭贏，XX 左右，敖悍騷裾，誅罰貨耐。丹省誤乳，（Strips 10）

固奪侵試。胡貉離絕，塚高棺柩。巴蜀筭竹，筐篋斂笥。（Strips 11）

The first chapter "X Lu"「X 祿」of the chapter of Cang Jie, in the rime category of Zhi 之 and Zhi 職, the characters rhyming with Zhi 之 are: Zhi 志, Ji 忌, Kai 欬, Jiu 久, Dai 戴, Jiu 舊, Si 思, Er 餌, Gai 該, Zai 載, Lai 睞, Cai 裁, Zi 字, You 右, Nai 耐, Jiu 柩, Si 笥. (Colored in yellow)

The first chapter "X Lu"「X 祿」of the chapter of Cang Jie, in the rime category of Zhi 之 and Zhi 職, the characters rhyming with Zhi 職 are: Zhi 職, De 得, Bei 北, Ji 亟, Chi 敕, Fu 服, Ce 廁, Yi 異, Zhi 織, Shi 試. (Colored in blue)

Since there were lots of variant Chinese characters, we would no longer list them in the article. However, we can see from the example that the written pattern was fixed and obvious. 4 characters were grouped in one sentence and the whole chapter repeated this writing pattern.

We agree with the opinion of scholar Hu Pingsheng about the wordbook in ancient times as the teaching material of literacy for entrance level; it should be read in catchy. However, as we can see the above characters of *the chapter of Cang Jieof the Han bamboo slip of Beijing University*, they are simply characters building up a sentence; some of them not only make no sense in the sentence but also make no sense to group words, no mention for us to understand the full text. Even scholar Zhu Fenghan 朱鳳瀚[30] gave comprehensive annotations for the raw strips, gave explanations for each character, and used interchangeable words (Different characters with similar pronunciation) to pronoun some characters and many other scholars such as scholar Hu Pingsheng,[31][32][33][34][35][36][37][38][39][40][41][42] Wang Ning,[43] Qin Hualin,[44] Ju

---

30 The Peking University Excavated Manuscript Research Center edited北京大學出土文獻研究所編, *Peking University Bamboo Strips of Xi Han*《北京大學藏西漢竹書》, Shanghai,Shanghai Guji Press,09/2015.

31 Hu Pingsheng胡平生, After Reading *Cang* 1 讀《蒼》劄記一, The research center of the newly excavated document of Fudan復旦大學出土文獻與古文字研究中心, 21/12/2015, http://www.gwz.fudan.edu.cn/Web/Show/2687

32 Hu Pingsheng胡平生, After Reading *Cang* 2讀《蒼》劄記二, The research center of the newly excavated document of Fudan 復旦大學出土文獻與古文字研究中心, 22/12/2015, http://www.gwz.fudan.edu.cn/Web/Show/2692

33 Hu Pingsheng 胡平生, After Reading *Cang* 3 讀《蒼》劄記三, The research center of the newly excavated document of Fudan復旦大學出土文獻與古文字研究中心, 23/12/2015, http://www.gwz.fudan.edu.cn/Web/Show/2693

34 Hu Pingsheng 胡平生, After Reading *Cang* 4讀《蒼》劄記四, The research center of the newly excavated document of Fudan 復旦大學出土文獻與古文字研究中心, 30/12/2015, http://www.gwz.fudan.edu.cn/Web/Show/2704

35 Hu Pingsheng 胡平生, After Reading *Cang* 5 讀《蒼》劄記五, The research center of the newly excavated document of Fudan 復旦大學出土文獻與古文字研究中心, 31/12/2015, http://www.gwz.fudan.edu.cn/Web/Show/2706

36 Hu Pingsheng 胡平生, After Reading *Cang* 6 讀《蒼》劄記六, The research center of the newly excavated document of Fudan 復旦大學出土文獻與古文字研究中心, 02/01/2016, http://www.gwz.fudan.edu.cn/Web/Show/2712

37 Hu Pingsheng 胡平生, After Reading *Cang* 7 讀《蒼》劄記七, The research center of the newly excavated document of Fudan 復旦大學出土文獻與古文字研究中心, 04/01/2016, http://www.gwz.fudan.edu.cn/Web/Show/2714

38 Hu Pingsheng 胡平生, After Reading *Cang* 8 讀《蒼》劄記八, The research center of the newly excavated document of Fudan 復旦大學出土文獻與古文字研究中心, 08/01/2016, http://www.gwz.fudan.edu.cn/Web/Show/2717

39 Hu Pingsheng 胡平生, After Reading *Cang* 9 讀《蒼》劄記九, The research center of the

Huanlin, [45] and He Yuhua [46] gave more possible supplementation and correction of the annotations, explanations and interchangeable words of the raw strips, still, *the chapter of Cang Jieof the Han bamboo slip of Beijing University* seems not readable enough in many ways and hard to be given a logical meaning of the literacy context through the whole chapter.

If we assume that the author of *the chapter of Cang Jie* was trying to help people to read and to write, then trying to collect as many character's fonts as possible and avoid the repetition for one character may be a

---

newly excavated document of Fudan 復旦大學出土文獻與古文字研究中心, 09/01/2016, http://www.gwz.fudan.edu.cn/Web/Show/2721

40 Hu Pingsheng 胡平生, After Reading *Cang* 10 讀《蒼》劄記十, The research center of the newly excavated document of Fudan 復旦大學出土文獻與古文字研究中心, 10/01/2016, http://www.gwz.fudan.edu.cn/Web/Show/2722

41 Hu Pingsheng 胡平生, After Reading *Cang* 11 讀《蒼》劄記十一, The research center of the newly excavated document of Fudan 復旦大學出土文獻與古文字研究中心, 15/01/2016, http://www.gwz.fudan.edu.cn/Web/Show/2727

42 Hu Pingsheng 胡平生, After Reading *Cang* 12 讀《蒼》劄記十二, The research center of the newly excavated document of Fudan 復旦大學出土文獻與古文字研究中心, 20/01/2016, http://www.gwz.fudan.edu.cn/Web/Show/2735

43 Wang Ning 王寧, Reading Han Scripts of Peking University of *Cang* 北大漢簡《蒼頡篇》讀劄（上）, The research center of the newly excavated document of Fudan 復旦大學出土文獻與古文字研究中心, 22/02/2016, http://www.gwz.fudan.edu.cn/Web/Show/2744

44 Qin Hualin秦樺林, Reading West-Han Scripts of Peking University of *Cang* 1北大藏西漢簡《倉頡篇》劄記（一）,JinboWang簡帛網, 14/11/2015, http://www.bsm.org.cn/show_article.php?id=2355

45 Ju Huanwen 鞠煥文, Reading Han Scripts of Peking University of *Cang* 1北大《倉頡篇》讀書劄記（一）, JnboWang簡帛網, 25/11/2015, http://www.bsm.org.cn/show_article.php?id=2377

46 He Yuhua 何餘華, Reading Han Scripts of Peking University of *Cang* 1北大藏漢簡《倉頡篇》研讀劄記（一）, JinboWang簡帛網, 04/12/2015, http://www.bsm.org.cn/show_article.php?id=2391

reasonable explanation of this situation. We may assume that the author used one different character with the same pronunciation to replace the already appeared character, so that, the teaching materials of literacy could have as many different characters as possible. If this hypothesis holds, it could explain many meaningless characters in the chapter were trying to use the same pronunciation for the students to pick up, but not the meaning of the character itself for students to learn in the sentence.

So, in the aspect of making annotation of *the chapter of Cang Jie of the Han bamboo slip of Beijing University*, things should be deemed separately: one is recognizing the character itself, and the other is to explain the words groped by the characters. The past situation may be the same as what we are facing now. The situation of the interchangeable words makes *the chapter of Cang Jie* more like a dictionary of Character than a logical book, which, on the other hand, made it a very typical wordbook in the ancient time of Qin and Han dynasty. If people of Pre-Han and Han want to learn how to read, they used a *chapter of Cang Jie* to pick up, pronounce, and to memorize the characters.

To understand, to read and to comprehend this newly excavated document is not an easy task at present. If we want to fully understand *the chapter of Cang Jie of the Han bamboo slips of Beijing University*, we may pay more attention of acknowledging the pronunciations of the characters, find out the different meaning for grouping the words with the same pronunciation, so that we could know the meaning of the word, rather than simply considering the exact meaning of the character within the words, the sentence, and chapter. Of course, since the antiquity of this long-lost document was found in recent years, the accuracy of the characters in the document is still needed to be researched. And we hope more documents could be unearthed to help us to further understand the situation during that time and more information could be found to build up a closer version of the original teaching materials of literacy at that time.

Chapter Six
The teaching material of Mathematics 數學教材

Math is an indispensable and necessary tool for human civilizations.[1] It is highly connected with every aspect of our daily life. In ancient China, math was a   kind of knowledge that the officials must acquire. However, we could only use the *Nine Chapters on the Art of Mathematics*《九章算術》, which was a math book written between B.C.100-A.D.100 in China, as the basic material to study the Chinese math education history.

From the handed-down materials, the earliest document of mathematic specialized book is *the Nine Chapters on the Art of Mathematics.*   As one of the ancient mathematic writings, it formed a systematic representation of Chinese classical mathematic writing. Academically, we generally recognize the content of *the Nine Chapters on the Art of Mathematics*as an epitomizedmathematical work in pre-Qin and Qin and Han dynasties based on its complete categories and rich content.

However, it is not easy to tell the proportion for the math content of Pre-Qin and Qin simply in   reading *the Nine Chapters on the Art of Mathematics*, and it is even harder to tell which part of them was   the math teaching materials and how the officials would use the math formulation to help to tackle the daily problem.

Nothing related to math can be found before that era. There are many

---

1   Adler, Philip J. and Pouwels, Randall L., *World Civilizations*, Wadsworth, Cengage Learning, 2012, pp. 23, 109.

theoretical assumptions about when *The Nine Chapters on the Art of Mathematics*was written; it seems more likely that   that it was written in the middle of the Western Han Dynasty or the early years of the Eastern Han Dynasty.[23]   Thanks to the newly excavated documents[4] found in recent decades, the knowledge of math education in ancient China could be greatly improved. In this chapter, the teaching material of mathematics around B.C.200 of China would be studied by using several newly excavated documents, and three empirical aspects of the mathematical knowledge of that period will be fully discussed. They are a) the teaching material of math for the management of land and taxation; b) the teaching material of math for the management of storage and goods and c) the teaching material of math for the management of labor and manufacture industry. With this in mind, our understanding of the application of empirical mathematics around B.C.200 China will be greatly enhanced.

In this chapter, the author would like to sort out the newly excavated documents related to mathematics education and discuss the teaching material of mathematics in Pre-Qin China structurally and systematically.

---

2   Li Di, *A concise history of Chinese Mathematics*, Shenyang, Liaoning People's Publishing House,1984,pp. 61-63.

3   Du Shiran, *Mathematics. History.Society*, Shenyang, Liaoning Education Press, 2003, pp. 33-36.

4   They include:
  The math material of Warring States bamboo slips of Tsinghua University
  The "9 9 formula" of Qin bamboo slips of Liye
  The Book of Calculation of Qin bamboo slips of Peking University
  The Shu/Number of the Qin bamboo slips of Academy of Yuelu
  The Book of Calculation of the Han bamboo slips of Zhangjiashan

6.1. The introduction of teaching materials of Math of Pre-Qin

After the chaotic war stage of the Qin Empire, a great number of documents were lost. Under this circumstance, to excavate, to supplement, and to make annotations of all kinds of documents has become a popular trend in the Han dynasty. In the field of math documents, the ancient one, including Zhang Cang 張蒼, Geng Shouchang 耿壽昌, Du Zhong 杜忠, Xu Shang 許商, Yin Xian 尹咸, Liu Xin 劉歆, who were described as "being good at using calculation and calendar", and who not only made supplementations for the math documents but also helped the intensity of those loosen knowledge of astronomy, calendar, manufacture, agriculture, and other aspects during the learning and teaching math.[5]

6.1.1. The handed-down documents of the teaching materials of Mathematics

Some of the most outstanding works were done in this atmosphere. Both the math book of the *Nine Chapters on the Art of Mathematics* and *the calculation book of Zhou Bi/Zhou Bi Suan Jing*《周髀》/《周髀算經》[6] from the handed-down documents are the most representative works in the

---

5   Wang Quan ed.王權主編, *History of Chinese primary school mathematics teaching*《中國小學 數學教學史》, Jinan, Shandong Education Publishing House, 1996, pp. 5-93.

6   *The calculation book of Zhou Bi/Zhou Bi Suan Jing*is one of the oldest math book of China. It is called *Zhou Bi* as well.   The book age is arguable; however, the content of the book is related to astronomical calendar. The English version of *Zhou Bi* can be found in Christopher Cellen, *Astronomy and mathematics in Ancient China: the Zhou bi suan jing*, Cambridge University Press,1995, Chapter 4, pp.171-205；also, Du Shiran estimated the time written of *Zhou bi* was around BC 100, see Du Shiran,*Mathematis. History.Society*,Shenyang, Liaoning Education Press, 2003, pp.25-28.

mathematics field within the Chinese classics during that time. The latest written time of these two books was reckoned during the semi-late Western Han period. Both of the books were well written and enjoyed high math quality, especially *the Nine Chapters on the Art of Mathematics*, with abundant contents and strict structures. After a thousand years of circulation, it is still an outstanding book compared with other handed down math books. It was a book written around the first century B.C. by an unknown author. Some scholars highly believed that *the Nine Chapters on the Art of Mathematics* was written by Ma xu 馬續.[7] And some scholars deduced it could be the work by Zhang Cang 張蒼 and Geng Shouchang 耿壽昌 through their prior work of reconstructing the burned math documents.[8] There are 9 chapters systematically divided into 246 math problem solutions. All 9 chapters are as the follows: chapter 1 with a content related to Fang Tian 方田 (rectangular fields); chapter 2 with a content related to Su Mi 粟米 (grains); chapter 3 with a content related to Cui Fen 衰分 (proportional distribution); chapter 4 with a content related to Shao Guang 少廣(small width); chapter 5 with a content related to Shang Gong 商功 (estimating workloads); chapter 6 with a content related to Jun Shu 均輸(equitable distribution); chapter 7 with a content related to Ying Bu Zu 盈不足 (excess and deficiency); chapter 8 with a content related to Fang Cheng 方程 (rectangular arrays); and chapter 9 with a content related to Gou Gu 勾股

7　Qian Baocong 錢寶琮, *History of Chinese Mathematics* 《中國數學史》, Beijing, Science Press, 1992, p.33.

8　Liu Hui劉徽annotation; Li Chunfeng李淳風notes and annotation; Guo Shuchun郭書春critical edition and translation; Joseph W. Daubwn 道本周 and Xu Yibao徐義保 English critical edition and translation, *Nine Chapters on the Art of Mathematics*, Shenyang, Liaoning Education Press, 2013, p.40.

(base and side of right triangles). The pattern of the book is based on each chapter introducing a question and then giving a math solution. Differentiating from the ancient Greek logic deduction, *the Nine Chapters on the Art of Mathematics* was not a theoretical system of mathematic book. As Professor Jaques Gernet pointed out, "at first sight, Chinese mathematics might be thought of as empirical and utilitarian since it contains nothing with which we are familiar; more often than not it contains no definitions, axioms, theorems or proofs."[9] That is the way of thinking in Chinese tradition. So, the book had a profound impact on the development and teaching of math education in ancient China.[10]

6.1.2.   The newly excavated documents of the teaching materials of Math

So, we could tell that the development of math was quite good during the written time of *the Nine Chapters on the Art of Mathematics,* which was dated in the middle of the Western Han dynasty. The transformation of the Qin and Han dynasties was tremendous. If we could find the real situation of math education, we would   be able to understand the formation period of the bureaucratic system of China.   What was the exact math education situation at this transitional period? Fortunately, some conversational issues of mathematics were sorted out from the newly excavated documents of Qin and early Han dynasties.   If we want to find out the teaching materials of math around B.C.200 China, there were quite many newly excavated documents related toit in recent years.

---

9   Jean-Claude Martzloff, *A History of Chinese Mathematics*, New York, Springer, 1995.

10   Wang Quan ed.王權主編, *History of Chinese primary school mathematics teaching* 《中國小學數學教學史》, Jinan, Shandong Education Publishing House, 1996,   p. 57.

These newly excavated documents were:

i   The math material of Warring States bamboo slips of Tsinghua University 清華大學戰國簡的數學史料;

The math material of Warring States bamboo slips of Tsinghua University is in the progress of organizing. Within one of the organized chapters, *the Form of Calculation/Suan Biao* 《算表》 was not discovered among other newly excavated documents. It was a small book with practicality for teaching calculation. The content of *the Form of Calculation/Suan Biao* is the extension of the Ninety – nine multiplication table.[11]

ii The "9 9 formula" of Qin bamboo slips of Liye 里耶秦簡"九九乘法表";[12]

iii *The Book of Calculation* of Qin bamboo slips of Peking University 北京大學藏秦簡《算書》;[13]

The content of *The Book of Calculation* of Qin bamboo slips of Peking University is mainly about the calculation of field, taxations, grains exchange, and other practical issues.

iv *TheShu/Number* of the Qin bamboo slips of Academy of Yuelu 嶽麓書院藏秦簡《數》;

---

11 Tsinghua University Unearthed Literature Research and Protection Center ed. 清華大學出土文獻研究與保護中心編, leaded by Li Xueqin李學勤主編, *Tsinghua University Collection of Warring States Bamboo Slips*, Vol. 4 《清華大學藏戰國竹簡（肆）》, Shanghai, East-west Book Co., 2013.

12 Chen Wei 陳偉, *Liye Qin bamboo slips: An annotated explanation* 《里耶秦簡牘校釋》, Wuhan, Wuhan University Press, 2012, p. 17.

13 Han Wei 韓巍, The mathematical resources of Qin bamboo slips collected by Peking University 北大秦簡中的數學文獻[J], *Cultural Relics*, 2012(6):85-89.

The basic situation of *the Shu/Number* of Qin bamboo slips of the Academy of Yuelu was well discussed by many scholars.[1415] Similarities and differences of the content between *TheShu/Number* of the Qin bamboo slips of Academy of Yuelu and *the Book of Calculation* of Qin bamboo slips of Peking University was research by scholar Chen Songchang in his article *the summary of the content of the Qin bamboo slips of Academy of Yuelu*.[16]

v   *The Book of Calculation* of the Han bamboo slips of Zhangjiashan 張家山漢墓竹簡《算數書》;[17]

In 2000, the organization team of the bamboo slips of Zhangjiashan published the first book of the explanatory note of the Book of Calculation[18]and in 2001 the whole version of the study and explanatory note of the Han bamboo slips of

14 Xiao Can 蕭燦, *The research of Mathematics of Qin bamboo slips collected by Yulu College*, Beijing, Social Sciences Academic Press, 2015.

15 Chen Songchang etc. 陳松長等, *The Compilation and Research of the Qin Bamboo Slips of Academy ofYuelu*《嶽麓書院藏秦簡的整理與研究》, Shanghai, Zhongxi Press, 2014.

16 Chen Songchang 陳松長, A Summarize of the Qin Slips Collected by Yuelu Academy嶽麓書院所藏秦簡綜述[J], *Cultural Relics*, 2009(3):75-88.

17 Chrispher Cellen, The Suàn shù shū̄ 算數書, "Writings on reckoning": Rewriting the history of early Chinese mathematics in the light of an excavated manuscript [J], *Historia Mathematica,* 2007(34): 10-44; a very concise explanatory note with Chinese version of *the Suàn shù shu* can also be found in Wang Wenjun ed., *Zhongguo shuxueshi daxi*, Supplementary vol.I, *Data of Mathematics in Early China*,Beijing Normal University Press, 2004, pp. 1-37.

18 Jiangling Study Group of the Jiangling Documents 江陵張家山漢簡整理小組, Transcription of Bamboo Suanshushu or A Book of Arithmetic江陵張家山竹簡《算數書》釋文[J], *Cultural Relics*, 2000(9):78-84.

Zhangjiashan was published.[19] A few years later, a revised study of the study and explanatory note of the Han bamboo slips of Zhangjiashan was published by the organization team of the bamboo slips of Zhangjiashan.[20] The main content of The Book of Calculation of the Han bamboo slips of Zhangjiashan could be divided into 2 parts, one was comprehensive research of mathematics and the other was a monographic study of mathematics.

In a simple way to explain the developments of math education, from the astronomical calendar to the taxation of agriculture, it was assumed that the ruler was eager to manipulate the society in a way, and math was a very good and straight forward tool to achieve this goal. Hence, if we want to talk about the teaching materials of mathematics around B.C. 200 China, a good way to do the research is to try to understand what daily issues would use math for a solution under the social system of prefectures and counties of a bureaucratic regime.

Many of the newly excavated documents mentioned above are still in the progress of researching and organizing. Quantities of articles and researches were done by different scholars, and based on these precious documents, if we try to resort the original situation of the math education in Pre-Qin China, we should understand a core point: the education of math during that time was based on the fact that people were trying to find a scientific way to tackle

---

19 Zhangjiashan Hanjian Group ed., *Tomb No. 247, The Han bamboo slips of Zhangjiashan*, Beijing, Cultural Relics Publishing House, 2001.

20 Zhangjiashan Hanjian Group, *Revised translation of Tomb No. 247, The Han bamboo slips of Zhangjiashan*, Beijing, Cultural Relics Publishing House, 2006.

their daily problems and the governments were trying to cope with the ruling problems with their subjects of a kingdom easier. In a simple way to explain the developments of math education, from the astronomical calendar to the taxation of agriculture, it was assumed that the rulers were eager to manipulate the society in a way, and math was a very good and straight forward tool to achieve this goal. Hence, if we want to talk about the teaching materials of mathematics of Pre-Qin China, a good way to do the research is to try to understand what daily issues would use math for a solution under the social system of prefectures and counties.

6.2. The classification of the teaching material of math
Three main categories of the teaching material of math around B.C. 200

The officials-learn-to-be had to learn enough mathematical skills and knowledge to deal with their working life; plebian had to learn enough mathematical skills and knowledge to deal with daily issues and even the priestling had to learn enough mathematic skill and knowledge to understand the astronomy and solar terms. After we go through the newly excavated documents related to teaching material of math, it is not hard to find out that the math documents mainly reflect three issues.

i   the management of land and taxation;

ii   the management of storage and goods;

iii the management of the labor and manufacturing industry.

For this matter of fact, the following sections would discuss the teaching materials of math around B.C. 200 China in terms of these issues.

6.2.1. The teaching material of math for the management of land and taxation

The Qin Law regulated the obligation of the official while dealing with the mathematic problem. If we want to talk about the most important daily issues for a county, it must be how to collect taxation. According *to Qin bamboo slips of Yunmeng Shuihudi, Qin bamboo slips of Yuelu,* and *Han bamboo slips of Zhangjiashan*, the government collected the tax based on the number of the land of the citizen. It was a major income for the state in an agricultural economy. Due to this condition, to measure and calculate the land area was a daily and important duty for the related departments, especially for the local sectors of Xian/prefecture 縣.[21]

From the handed-down documents, Qin Empire united China and Qin Empire united the unit converter and measurements of length, capacity, and weight. Among the newly excavated documents, *the statutes concerning Checkingof the Qin bamboo slips of Yunmeng Shuihudi* shows us that there will be punishments for the officials if they wrongly measure the grains.[22] And the Qin law gave such precise regulation to guide the official to do the checking of so many aspects of the society, which was truly impressive. To be sure, this reflected the severe law management was not just used to punish the citizen or plebian, and even the official also faced strict retains of the law under the policy made by Legalists' School.

---

21 Xian/prefecture 縣 was the local sector under the social structure transforming from the feudal patrimonial system to the prefectures and counties system.

22 Huleswe,A.F.P. *Remnants of Ch'in Law: An Annotated Translation of the Ch'in Legal and Administrative Rules of the 3rd Century B.C. Discovered in Yün-meng Prefecture, Hu-pei Province, in 1975.* Brill, Leiden, E. J. Brill Publisher, 1985, pp. 93-101.

In *the Shu/Number* of the Qin bamboo slips of Academy of Yuelu, the bamboo slips of No. 0458 were the mathematical conversion of weight: 16 Liang 兩 equals to 1 Jin 斤, 30 Jin 斤 equals to 1 Jun 鈞, 4 Jun 鈞 equals to 1 Dan 石.[23]

There were unified unit converters of weight and capacity about the grains.

The unit converter of weightsin Qin		
Dan 石	120 Jin 斤	1920 Liang 兩
Ban Dan/half of Dan 半石	60 Jin 斤	960 Liang 兩
Jun 鈞	30 Jin 斤	480 Liang 兩
	1 Jin 斤	16 Liang 兩

Fig 6.1. [24]

The unit converter of capacitiesin Qin		
Tong/Bucket 桶	10 Dou 斗	100 Sheng/liter 升
	Dou 斗	1 Sheng/liter 升
Can 參		3 1/3 Sheng/liter 升

Fig 6.2. [25]

The people of Qin were using the elaborated math knowledge to solve the daily problem, thanks to the ancients' wisdom and we believe that the

---

23 Xiao Can蕭燦, *The research of Mathematics of Qin bamboo slips collected by Yulu College*, Social Sciences Academic Press, Beijing, 2015, p.65.

24 Xiao Can蕭燦, *The research of Mathematics of Qin bamboo slips collected by Yulu College*, Social Sciences Academic Press, Beijing, 2015, p.65.

25 Xiao Can蕭燦, *The research of Mathematics of Qin bamboo slips collected by Yulu College*, Social Sciences Academic Press, Beijing, 2015.

public and private education have made   great efforts about it.

In t*he Statutes on Agriculture of the Qin bamboo slips of Yunmeng Shuihudi*, the officials have to know the math to collect taxation: "the delivery of hay and straw per Qing 頃 is to be done according to the number of fields bestowed. Irrespective of whether the fields are cultivated or uncultivated the delivery per Qing is three bushels of hay (or) two bushels of straw. From a ranking of hay or a bundle of whitlow grass upward, everything will be received."[26] The regulation of this matter was the same as the Han dynasty according to the *Han bamboo slips of Zhangjiashan*. Because the shape and size of the cultivated land were not the same, the computational formula of the unit area could not be thoroughly applied. When dealing with taxation of the land, official often used Ping fang bu/square step 平方步 as the area measurement, and the converting metric between Qing 頃 and Mu 畝 was highly necessary. Except for the converting metric between Qing 頃 and Mu 畝 was necessary, there were other different cases which needed mathematical conversion.　One example was that under the diversecondi- tions of the land, climate, and planting habits, the variety of the grain paid by farmers as taxation was different. The official might learn the math skill to unify the monetary equivalent of the grains.　In *the Statutes on Agriculture of the Qin bamboo slips of Yunmeng Shuihudi*, some scholars gave annotations for the original article as "after the hay and straware collected, (the hay and straw) could be weighed and transported." 入芻稾，相輸度，

---

26 Huleswe, A.F.P. *Remnants of Ch'in Law: An Annotated Translation of the Ch'in Legal and Administrative Rules of the 3rd Century B.C. Discovered in Yün-meng Prefecture, Hu-pei Province, in 1975.* Brill, Leiden, E. J. Brill Publisher, 1985, p.23.

可燼也[27]; some considered it differently by saying the meaning of the original text should be "when delivering hay and straw, the substitution of the one of the other is allowed."[28] As far as the author concerned, the explanation of the hay and straw could be substituted for one another was more close to the actual situation during that time. Because in the practical situation of paying taxation, the mathematical conversion of grains was needed for the official and making   this into the law was reasonable.

In other newly excavated documents, we could also find materials of math dealing with a special case of taxation and land.

In *the Shu/Number* of the Qin bamboo slips of the Academy of Yuelu, the bamboo slips of No. 0887 and bamboo slips of No. 0537[29] were examples to teach people how to measure land and calculate taxation. In the meanwhile, whit the bamboo slips of No. 0887 and bamboo slips of No. 0537, it could explain and answer for the bamboo slips of No. 9055. The bamboo slips of No. 9055 raise a question about how to calculate the field area with 1 Dou 鬥 of dry hay and using the way given from the bamboo slips of No. 0887 and bamboo slips of No. 0537, the math problem could be solved with a result of 5 and 5/9 steps.[30]

---

27 Theorganization team of bamboo slips of Qin tomb of Shuihudi 睡虎地秦墓竹簡整理小組, *Bamboo slips of Qin tomb of Shuihudi*《睡虎地秦墓竹簡》, Beijing, Cultural Relics Press, 1978. p. 28.

28 Huleswe,A.F.P. *Remnants of Ch'in Law: An Annotated Translation of the Ch'in Legal and Administrative Rules of the 3rd Century B.C. Discovered in Yün-meng Prefecture, Hu-pei Province, in 1975.* Brill, Leiden, E. J. Brill Publisher, 1985, p.23.

29 Xiao Can蕭燦, *The research of Mathematics of Qin bamboo slips collected by Yulu College*, Social Sciences Academic Press, Beijing, 2015. p.28.

30 Xiao Can蕭燦, *The research of Mathematics of Qin bamboo slips collected by Yulu College*, Beijing,Social Sciences Academic Press, 2015, p.28.

6.2.2. The teaching material of math for the management of storage and goods

There was meticulous regulation of the management of storage and goods in the newly excavated documents of Qin. It was incarnated in *the Statutes on Granaries* and *the statutes concerning Checking* of *the Qin bamboo slips of Yunmeng Shuihudi.*

The total amounts of the grains, hay, and other taxations paid by the farmers were in huge numbers. To put them into storage, to allocate and transport them, and to distribute them were miscellaneous jobs for the officials in charge. Normally, there would be granaries for each prefecture according to the law of Qin. In *the Statutes on Granaries* of *the Qin bamboo slips of Yunmeng Shuihudi*, the newly excavated documents said: "when the grain in the year is entered in a granary, 10,000 bushels make one pile; they are ranged to form a 'house'……in Yueyang 櫟陽 20,000 bushels from one stack. In Xianyang 咸陽 100,000 bushels from one stack."[31] In most places, 10,000 bushels make one pile and each pile should be separated by a fence, but in the place of Yueyang, the unit for one stack to separate was 20,000 bushels and in the place of Xianyang, the unit for one stack to separate was 100,000 bushels. We believe these differences were based on the specific analysis of the actual condition for the taxation, granaries, and manpower. Practically, the calculation of the grains was using the measurement of volume. In the *Book of Calculation* of the Han bamboo slips

---

31 Huleswe,A.F.P. *Remnants of Ch'in Law: An Annotated Translation of the Ch'in Legal and Administrative Rules of the 3rd Century B.C. Discovered in Yün-meng Prefecture, Hu-pei Province, in 1975.* Brill, Leiden, E. J. Brill Publisher, 1985, pp.34-37.

of Zhangjiashan, there were cases about how to settle the problems of storage of grains and hay. The slip of Xuanlv 旋粟[32] was teaching how to calculate the volume of a pile of grains by giving formula of conical.   The high of the conical of the grains is 5 Chi 尺 (Chinese feet), the length of the circumference of the grain is 3 Zhang 丈 (10 Chinese feet), the volume of the pile is 125 (cubic) Chi.   2 Chi 尺 7 Cun 寸(inch, 0.1 Chinese feet) is 1 Dan 石(120 Chinese Jin 斤), the weight of the grain is 46 Dan 石 and 8 of the 27 Dan 石.[33]   The slip of Chu(芻, hay),[34] was teaching hot to settle the volume problem of hay.[35]   And the formulas of calculation solid geometry were the same with the handed-down documents of *the Nine Chapters on the Art of Mathematics*.   In *the Shu/Number* of the Qin bamboo slips of Academy of Yuelu, similar math questions and solutions related to how to weight storage and goods using the way of volume measurement.

For the high capacity granaries as much as 10 thousand Shi or even 100 thousand Shi, to measure the total weight of the grains and hay using the standard of volume instead of weighing them one by one, was a very scientific and convenient solution. The people and the officials at that time could use math knowledge wisely.   Through the newly excavated documents of math, it was not hard to predict that, the officials in charge of the granaries

---

32   Peng Hao 彭浩,*An annotated explanation on the Book of Calculation of the Han bamboo slips of Zhangjiashan*張家山漢簡《算數書》注釋, Beijing, Science Press, 2011, p.105.

33   Zhangjiashan Hanjian Group ed., *Revised translation of Tomb No. 247, The Han bamboo slips of Zhangjiashan*, Beijing, Cultural Relics Publishing House, 2006, p.151.

34   Zhangjiashan Hanjian Group ed., *Revised translation of Tomb No. 247, The Han bamboo slips of Zhangjiashan*, Beijing, Cultural Relics Publishing House, 2006, p.151.

35   Peng Hao 彭浩,*An annotated explanation on the Book of Calculation of the Han bamboo slips of Zhangjiashan*張家山漢簡《算數書》注釋, Beijing, Science Press, 2011, p.104.

would normally use the volume measurement method for the big amount of taxation and weight measurement method for the small amount.　The bulk of hay and straw were always big, which made the weight of them hard to process; the volume measurement method would be used to weigh　the hay and straw in most of the cases. As to the daily miscellaneous work, such as paying checks or giving food, it would be easier to weigh the grain directly.

There was guidance for the exchange of food supplies. As a variety of grains, people sometimes had to use one kind of grain to exchange other kinds of grain. And *the Shu/Numberof the Qin bamboo slips of the Academy of Yuelu* gave us examples about how to solve the application problem of linear equations in two unknowns about the exchange of different kinds of grains.

The bamboo slips of No.0971:[36] using rice 米 to exchange wheat 麥 divided by 2 and multiplied 3 (wheat = rice ÷ 2 X 3). Using wheat to exchange rice, divided by 3 and multiplied 2 (rice = wheat ÷3 X 2). Using millet 粟 to exchange wheat, divided by 10 and multiplied 9 (wheat = millet ÷10 X 9). Using wheat to exchange millet, divided by 9 and multiplied 10 (millet = wheat÷9 X 10).

The bamboo slips of No.0823:[37] using rice to exchange millet, be divided by 3 and multiplied 5 (millet = rice ÷3 X 5). Using millet to exchange rice, divided by 5 and multiplied 3 (rice = millet ÷5 X 3). Using polished rice 粺 to exchange rice, divided by 9 and multiplied 10 (polished rice = rice ÷9

36　Xiao Can蕭燦, *The research of Mathematics of Qin bamboo slips collected by Yulu College*, Beijing, Social Sciences Academic Press, 2015. p.67.

37　Xiao Can蕭燦, *The research of Mathematics of Qin bamboo slips collected by Yulu College*, Beijing,Social Sciences Academic Press, 2015. p.67.

X 10). Using rice to exchange polished rice, divided by 10 and multiplied 9 (rice= polished rice ÷ 10 X 9).

The bamboo slips of No.0853:[38] using polished rice to exchange millet, divided by 27 and multiplied 50 (millet = polished rice ÷ 27 X 50). Using millet to exchange polished rice, divided by 50 and multiplied 27 (polished rice = millet ÷50 X 27). Using well-polished rice 毇 to exchange rice, divided by 8 and multiplied 10 (rice = well-polished rice ÷8 X 10). Using rice to exchange well-polished rice, divided by 10 and multiplied 8 (well-polished rice = rice ÷ 10 X 8).

There were lots of application problems of the exchange among storages similar to the above 3 examples of *the Shu/Numberof the Qin bamboo slips of Academy of Yuelu*, and all of them were math solution of linear equation in two unknowns. The math education for the people of Qin was advanced. The way to solve the linear equation in two unknowns was used in all kinds of problems.

6.2.3. The teaching material of math for the management of labor and manufacture industry

The advanced productive forces were controlled by the rulers in ancient times. For the reason to produce all kinds of specialized goods for the aristocracy and government, many specific industries were managed by the government. In order to manage the manufacturing industry and to develop the production level, production engineering had to be upgraded with the help

---

38 Xiao Can蕭燦, *The research of Mathematics of Qin bamboo slips collected by Yulu College,* Beijing,Social Sciences Academic Press, 2015. pp.67-68.

of the education of math. The official had to acquire enough math knowledge to deal with their work. We could find different officials had to have different math skills through the newly excavated documents. Those officials who in charge of the industry of copper money casting, had to know how to calculate the loss of copper; those official salt comprador had to be familiar with the accounting of salt; those officials who in charge of the textile industry had to learn the efficiency of weaving and the gradient of the raw silk and bright silk. The industries were separated in detail, in *Qin bamboo slips of Yunmeng Shuihudi,* we already found regulations for managing different aspects of various industry. For example, *the Statutes on Artisans* were the regulation of the official handicraft industry; statutes of *the Statutes on Norms for Artisans* were the regulation of the allotment standard ration of official production; *the Statutes on Equalization Artisans* were the regulation of scheduling the workers of handicraft industry.

In the *Book of Calculation* of the *Han bamboo slips of Zhangjiashan,* we could find out some math problem related tothe manufacturing industry, including "consuming copper 銅耗", "silk refining 絲煉", "trading salt 賈鹽", and so on.

Take "consuming copper 銅耗" and "silk refining 絲煉" as an example. "Consuming copper 銅耗": at that time, in the calculation instruction, making 1 Dan of copper would consume 7 Jin and 8 Liang. The math question of it in *the Calculation of theHan bamboo slips of Zhangjiashan* was: if there was 1 Jin 8 Liang 8 Zhu 銖 of copper, how many would be consumed? The math solution is given by the book: 1 Liang 12 and a half Zhu. The formula for calculating the consuming copper was given by the newly excavated document of *the Calculation.*[39]

"Silk refining 絲煉": it meant making raw silk into boiled silk. There were 16 Liang of raw silk, after boiling it and degumming, there would be 12 Liang of refining silk. The proportion of the transformation of silk refining was 16:12.[40]

The examples were very typical teaching materials of math by giving questions, solutions, and formula. No matter consuming copper, refining silk, or other daily life activities, the usages of mathematics were infiltrated into all kinds of industries. In another perspective, people did understand the knowledge of mathematics and it reflected that math education was at a complicated and precise level.

Many of the newly excavated documents mentioned above are still in the progress of researching and organizing. Quantities of articles and researches were done by different scholars, based on these precious documents, if we try to resort the original situation of the math education around B.C.200 China, we should understand a core point: the education of math during that time was based on the fact that people were trying to find a scientific way to tackle their daily problems and the governments were trying to cope with the ruling problems with their subjects more easily. In the entire newly excavated documents related to whit mathematical problems, we could find during that time, around B.C. 200, the math education had already achieved an outstanding level.

---

[39] Zhangjiashan Hanjian Group ed., *Revised translation of Tomb No. 247, The Han bamboo slips of Zhangjiashan*,Beijing, Cultural Relics Publishing House, 2006, p.138.

[40] Zhangjiashan Hanjian Group ed., *Revised translation of Tomb No. 247, The Han bamboo slips of Zhangjiashan*,Beijing, Cultural Relics Publishing House, 2006, p.142.

Chapter Seven

The ethical teaching material of *the Way to Be a Good Official* 道德教材

Different kinds of newly excavated documents, including law learning materials, literacy material, and mathematic materials, were discussed in the previous chapters. However, another kind of bamboo strips of teaching material was found in the tomb of Xi, under the belly of the corpse, in Yunmeng Shuihudi. It was titled as *The Way to Be a Good Official*《為吏之道》.

Since the discovery of *the bamboo slips of Yungmeng Shuihudi* in 1985, the study of "the way to be a good official" has been researched in various ways.

There are a few studies related to *The Way to Be a Good Official* based on the newly excavated document and handed-down materials. To meet the needs of the transformation from aristocracy 貴族制 to bureaucracy 官僚制 and from feudal patrimonial system 分封制 to the prefecture-county system 郡縣制, Qin needed to develop a group of materials for officials to learn to better their work. In the perspective of education, one way was that Qin made a serial of legislation and implements the policy of "law as education" 以法為教 and "officials as teachers" 以吏為師; the other was enforcing the control on the ethical issue of officials. As a blueprint of the ethical education of officials, we could find a group of newly excavated documents related to *The Way to Be a Good Official*. Except for *Qin bamboo slips of Yunmeng Shuihudi* was excavated *the Way to Be a Good Official* 《為吏之道》 as the ethical learning materials, *the Qin bamboo slips of Yuelu* 岳麓秦簡 was excavated *to Be an Official and the People*《為吏治官及黔首》.[1] And *the Qin bamboo slips of Beijing University* 北大藏秦簡 also was excavated document *The Book of Being Official*《從政之經》[2] which is related to the ethical learning materials for the official.

In the meanwhile, "the way to be a good official" is an important historical and legal topic in the research of ancient official administration. It was well researched. After the publication of *Bamboo slips of Qin tomb of Shuihudi*《睡虎地秦墓竹簡》, which was written by the Organization team of bamboo slips of Qin tomb of Shuihudi, different studies were made. Some scholars did some research by analyzing The Way to Be a Good Official character by character trying to come out with a comprehensive annotation of *The Way to Be a Good Official.*[3] Some argued the accuracy of the explanation of the annotation.[4] Some scholars concluded the influence of *The Way to Be a Good Official* in the federal field in ancient China.[5][6] Some

1 Chen Songchang etc. 陳松長等, *The Compilation and Research of the Qin Bamboo Slips of Academy of Yuelu*《嶽麓書院藏秦簡的整理與研究》, Shanghai, Zhongxi Press, 2014. pp.127-133.

2 Zhu Fenghan朱鳳瀚, Introduction of Cong Zheng Zhi Jing of Qin Bamboo Slips of Peking University北大藏秦簡《從政之經》述要[J], *Cultural Relics*, 2012(6):74-80.

3 Theorganization team of bamboo slips of Qin tomb of Shuihudi 睡虎地秦墓竹簡整理小組, *Bamboo slips of Qin tomb of Shuihudi*《睡虎地秦墓竹簡》, Beijing, Cultural Relics Press, 1978.

4 Bai Yulan 白于藍, Reading Notes on the text "*Wei Li Zhi Dao*為吏之道"of the Shuihudi Qin Dynasty Bamboo Strip Manuscripts 睡虎地秦簡《為吏之道》校讀劄記 [J], *Jianghan Archaeology*《江漢考古》, 2010 (3):125-131.

5 Zhu Zhenghui朱振輝, The Characteristic of Ruling of Official: from *the Way to Be a Good Official* of Qin Bamboo slips從秦簡《為吏之道》看秦國的吏治特色[J], *Journal of Historical Science*《史學月刊》, 2011(9):129-131.

did comparative studies by comparing the material of *The Way to Be a Good Official* of the Qin bamboo slips of Yunmeng Shuihudi and the material of *to be an Official and the People* of the Qin bamboo slips of Yuelu, trying to find out the meaning of the words and sentences. Some of them researched the importance of it through the development of intellectual history with China.[7] And some compared the articles of different excavated documents and tried to sort out the details within the articles among the bamboo slips.[8]

However, with several studies, few do the research under the perspective of teaching materials. In this chapter, the author would like to sort out the content of "the way to be a good official" of *Qin bamboo slips of Yunmeng Shuihudi* and try to analyze the importance of it under the perspective of teaching materials.

7.1. The main content of the teaching material of *the Way to Be a Good Official*

The whole set of the bamboo slips of *The Way to Be a Good Official* was found lying under the belly of the corpse of Xi in the tomb of Yunmeng

---

6   Li Ping 李平, An Analysis of the Theoretical Dilemma of the Rule of Law of Qin Dynasty——Focusing on *Yu Shu&Wei Li zhi Dao* of Shuihudi Qin Bamboo Texts 秦"法治"的理論困境透析——以水壺地秦簡《語書》、《為吏之道》為中心 [J], *Academic Exploration*《學術探索》, 2010(11):28-31.

7   Chen Zhanfeng 陳戰峰, The Development of Qin Thought and Culture Reflected by Shuihudi Qin Bamboo Slips *The Way To Be An Official* (Li) 從睡虎地秦簡《為吏之道》看秦思想文化的發展 [J], *Journal of Xidian University (Social Science Edition)*西安電子科技大學學報, 2004(2):65-68.

8   Chen Songchang etc. 陳松長等, *The Compilation and Research of the Qin Bamboo Slips of Academy of Yuelu*《嶽麓書院藏秦簡的整理與研究》, Shanghai, Zhongxi Press, 2014.

Shuihudi. There were 51 strips in total.[9] This group of bamboo slips was scratched in separated 5 rubrics. "From stains on most of the strips it is clear that they were held together by 3 sets of strings: close to the top and the bottom, and in the middle. Faint horizontal knife scratches over each of the 5 rubrics show, that the strips had been prepared before the received the writing."[10] The scratches of the last 2 rubrics were comparatively hasty and careless; it was highly possible that they were replenished.[11]

7.1.1. The ethical teaching materials of *The Way to Be a Good Official* by 5 good and the 5 wrong for officials

In the bamboo slips of *The Way to Be a Good Official,* 5 kinds of benignity well-doings were categorized as the good for being an official. There were 5 kinds of good for being an official; it should be rewarded once an official could achieve them:[12]

1. The first one is thathe should be royal and respect the superiors;

2. The second one is that he should be free from corruption and not to be costliness extravagance;

---

9   The organization team of bamboo slips of Qin tomb of Shuihudi 睡虎地秦墓竹簡整理小組, *Bamboo slips of Qin tomb of Shuihudi*《睡虎地秦墓竹簡》, Beijing, Cultural Relics Press, 1978. p.280.

10 A.F.P. Huleswe, *Remnants of Ch'in Law: An Annotated Translation of the Ch'in Legal and Administrative Rules of the 3rd Century B.C. Discovered in Yun-meng Prefecture*, Hu-pei Province, in 1975, Leiden,   E. J. Brill Publisher, 1985, p.208.

11 The organization team of bamboo slips of Qin tomb of Shuihudi 睡虎地秦墓竹簡整理小組, *Bamboo slips of Qin tomb of Shuihudi*《睡虎地秦墓竹簡》, Beijing, Cultural Relics Press, 1978. p.281.

12 The organization team of bamboo slips of Qin tomb of Shuihudi 睡虎地秦墓竹簡整理小組, *Bamboo slips of Qin tomb of Shuihudi*《睡虎地秦墓竹簡》, Beijing, Cultural Relics Press, 1978. p.283.

3. The third one is that he should judge properly;

4. The fourth one is that he should have acts of kindness;

5. The fifth one is that he should be respectful and humble.

5 kinds of fault beings were categorized as the wrong for being an official. And different kinds of wrong behaviors were separated into 3 groups.

There were 5 kinds of wrongdoings for being an official in the first group:[13]

1. The firstone is that he is over the limit of extravagance (is wrong);

2. The second firstone is that he is over the limit of arrogance (is wrong);

3. The third firstone is that he makes judgments without authorization (is wrong);

4. The fourth firstone is that he offends the superior without knowing the risk harm (is wrong);

5. The fifth firstone is that he looks down at people and looks high atthe money (is wrong).

There were 5 kinds of wrongdoings for being an official in the second group:[14]

1. The firstone is that he gets on people with arrogance (is wrong);

2. The second one is that he discontent with his time (is wrong);

3. The third one is that he seizes by force with his official position (is wrong);

---

13 The organization team of bamboo slips of Qin tomb of Shuihudi 睡虎地秦墓竹簡整理小組, *Bamboo slips of Qin tomb of Shuihudi*《睡虎地秦墓竹簡》, Beijing, Cultural Relics Press, 1978. pp.283-284.

14 The organization team of bamboo slips of Qin tomb of Shuihudi 睡虎地秦墓竹簡整理小組, *Bamboo slips of Qin tomb of Shuihudi*《睡虎地秦墓竹簡》, Beijing, Cultural Relics Press, 1978. pp.283-284.

4. The fourth one is that he takes orders disrespectfully (is wrong);

5. The fifth one is that he reconciles with his family but neglects his feudal position (is wrong).

There were 5 kinds of wrongdoings for being an official in the last group:[15]

1. The first one is that he gives unprincipled protection to the close ones, and this behavior would cause others' resentment;

2. The second one is that he makes use of authority wrongfully, and this behavior would lead to abuse his power to pursue personal interests;

3. The third one is that he does   things improperly, and this behavior would treat people without proper respect;

4. The fourth one is that he talks too much and act not enough, and this behavior would make people not close to you;

5. The fifth one is that he reproaches the superior/ruler, and this behavior would cause him to be killed.

The first rule for well-being was: to stay loyal; also, offending the superior was a wrong-being. The request for the obedience of the official was highly needed.[16] The author agreed with the view that *the Way to Be a Good Official,* as an ethical educational document for federal levels, was trying to build up the monarchical power under the circumstance of the social transformation.

---

15 The organization team of bamboo slips of Qin tomb of Shuihudi 睡虎地秦墓竹簡整理小組, *Bamboo slips of Qin tomb of Shuihudi*《睡虎地秦墓竹簡》, Beijing, Cultural Relics Press, 1978. pp.283-284.

16 Wang Huaping 王化平, *The Search of the Way of Being an Official in Qin Dynasty Unearthed at Yumeng and the Related Questions*《秦簡〈為吏之道〉及相關問題研究》[D], Chengdu, Sichuan University, 05/2003, p.6.

7.1.2.   The ethical teaching materials of *The Way to Be a Good Official* by the request of integrity

Except for the categorized 5 kinds of good and 5 kinds of wrong, there was more ethical guidance in the materials for the official. We are going to further discuss it   in different parts.

7.1.2.1.   To be incorruptible, selfless and to be willing to suffer poverty and unwilling to leave the right track

Concerning the self- cultivation culture of an official, being incorruptible, and selfless was the first ethical re-equipment. The beginning content of *the Way to Be a Good Official* was: "The way for being a good official, must be sinless and integrity, cautious and tough, to judge selflessly and to observe carefully, do not be strict, to judge the awards and punishments rigorously."[17] The core for educating the ethical official started with teaching them to get rid of the selfish needs and   not do anything corruptive. In the meanwhile, other parts of *the Way to Be a Good Official* also mentioned another way of the importance of incorruptible and selfless. Such as: "Quit it, quit it, the wealth should not be taken."[18] "When you see the money, do not take it and make you rich."[19] Since a good official should

---

17 The organization team of bamboo slips of Qin tomb of Shuihudi 睡虎地秦墓竹簡整理小組, *Bamboo slips of Qin tomb of Shuihudi*《睡虎地秦墓竹簡》, Beijing, Cultural Relics Press, 1978. p.281.

18 The organization team of bamboo slips of Qin tomb of Shuihudi 睡虎地秦墓竹簡整理小組, *Bamboo slips of Qin tomb of Shuihudi*《睡虎地秦墓竹簡》, Beijing, Cultural Relics Press, 1978. p.284.

19 The organization team of bamboo slips of Qin tomb of Shuihudi 睡虎地秦墓竹簡整理小組, *Bamboo slips of Qin tomb of Shuihudi*《睡虎地秦墓竹簡》, Beijing, Cultural Relics Press, 1978. p.284.

not be corrupted, while facing poverty, they should have a higher mind to keep themselves on the right track instead of being deluded by selfish desire. So, the *Way to Be a Good Official* talked about this situation by saying: "if an official wants to be rich badly, then he would not get it and be poor; if an official wants to be valuable badly, then he would not get it and be cheap. Do not adore rich, do not resent poor, practice, and be upright, bad things would go and good luck remains."[20]

7.1.2.2. To use appropriate attitude　to do judging and inspecting

We discussed in the previous chapters that, "law as education" 以法為教, was an indispensable policy for officials to implement. Similarly, one wanted to be a qualified official should have relevant skills and ability to teach the law to the people. Making a suitable and fair judge would always make a good example for the people. In this case, to be a good official must be capable to make good judge using the law.

The character "審" which was scratched on the bamboo slips was used 7 times in the bamboo slips of the *Way to Be a Good Official*, it means to judge or to inspect, and anyway, both of the meanings of "審" were to review things thoroughly, to think cases carefully and to implement the work fully.[21] This word was emphasized so many times, and it was used : "to judge/to inspect selflessly";[22] "to judge/to inspect the awards and punishments rigorously";[23]

20　The organization team of bamboo slips of Qin tomb of Shuihudi 睡虎地秦墓竹簡整理小組, *Bamboo slips of Qin tomb of Shuihudi*《睡虎地秦墓竹簡》, Beijing, Cultural Relics Press, 1978. p.282.

21　Li Xun 李恂, The Research of "Wei Li Zhi Dao" in Qin Dynasty Depending on the Unearthed Qin Jian 《以出土秦簡看秦代"為吏之道"》[D], Jinzhou, Bohai Uniersity, 05/2018, p.10.

22　Theorganization team of bamboo slips of Qin tomb of Shuihudi 睡虎地秦墓竹簡整理小組,

"to judge/to inspect wisely and knowing the capacity of people";[24] "to judge by listening, seeing and talking";[25] "while meeting things, to judge/to inspect properly";[26] "capable to judge like this";[27] and the last one "capable to judge/to inspect for the people".[28] It was a time the ruler of Qin trying to rule the state using the law from the way given by the Legalists. The law should be implemented properly in the society so that, it required the officials to know the law intimately and use the law to judge carefully. Even though *the Way to Be a Good Official* was an ethical blueprint for the officials to follow, we could still tell the influence of the legalism. If the government tried to run the society in a fictional order, there was no way an official would issue a regulation/ an order in the morning and rescind in the evening. The repeated

---

Bamboo slips of Qin tomb of Shuihudi《睡虎地秦墓竹簡》, Beijing, Cultural Relics Press, 1978. p.281.

23 Theorganization team of bamboo slips of Qin tomb of Shuihudi 睡虎地秦墓竹簡整理小組, *Bamboo slips of Qin tomb of Shuihudi*《睡虎地秦墓竹簡》, Beijing, Cultural Relics Press, 1978. p.281.

24 Theorganization team of bamboo slips of Qin tomb of Shuihudi 睡虎地秦墓竹簡整理小組, *Bamboo slips of Qin tomb of Shuihudi*《睡虎地秦墓竹簡》, Beijing, Cultural Relics Press, 1978. p.281.

25 Theorganization team of bamboo slips of Qin tomb of Shuihudi 睡虎地秦墓竹簡整理小組, *Bamboo slips of Qin tomb of Shuihudi*《睡虎地秦墓竹簡》, Beijing, Cultural Relics Press, 1978. p.281.

26 Theorganization team of bamboo slips of Qin tomb of Shuihudi 睡虎地秦墓竹簡整理小組, *Bamboo slips of Qin tomb of Shuihudi*《睡虎地秦墓竹簡》, Beijing, Cultural Relics Press, 1978. p.281.

27 Theorganization team of bamboo slips of Qin tomb of Shuihudi 睡虎地秦墓竹簡整理小組, *Bamboo slips of Qin tomb of Shuihudi*《睡虎地秦墓竹簡》, Beijing, Cultural Relics Press, 1978. p.281.

28 Theorganization team of bamboo slips of Qin tomb of Shuihudi 睡虎地秦墓竹簡整理小組, *Bamboo slips of Qin tomb of Shuihudi*《睡虎地秦墓竹簡》, Beijing, Cultural Relics Press, 1978. p.282.

appearance of "審", might tell us in a way that, in the legal level of Qin, the requirement for the official to implement regulation during daily work and teach the law to the plebian was high.[29]

Like what was showed by "審", *the Way to Be a Good Official*, as an ethical teaching material, echo the needs for officials to implement the policy of "law as education" 以法為教.

7.1.2.3. To be the role model for the people

Since one of the most important educational policies of Qin, was "officials as teachers" 以吏為師, if one wanted to be a good official, he should be a role model for his people. Even though the law of Qin was severe and the punishments were heavy, *the Way to Be a Good Official* still emphasized the critical needs for officials to behave themselves and keep close to the people. The author wonder, to hold gentle kindness was more or less antinomy with the thought of the Legalist's School. Han Fei had an important theory to unify the laws, statecrafts, and positions. It was the nature of humans. Han Fei considered the human nature was egoistic 自私自利. In his point of view, human beings were selfish and were all trying to make a profit off them and trying to not be harmed by others 趨利避害.[30] All the doctrines of Legalist's school he made were based on this opinion. It was hard to understand under the guide of Legalist's School, there would be ethical materials for officials to remind them to be kind to the people. And

---

29 Xu Weimin徐衛民& He ruikun賀潤坤, *Brief Introduction of the political thoughts of Qin*《秦政治思想述略》, Xi'an, Shangxi People's Education Press, 1995.

30 〔Warring States〕Han Fei〔戰國〕韓非, translated in to English by W.K.Liao, translated in to modern Chinese by Zhang Jue張覺, *Han Fei Zi*《韓非子》, Beijing, The Commercial Press, 2015.

this would open a question for us to further study.

However, back to the documents written here and based on the fact of the newly excavated documents found by *the Way to Be a Good Official*, the official "should be kind to his people and should not bully them";[31] "get rid of the bad and make the good thrive, love all the people. (if the people have) no sin, no sin, (the people should be) remit."[32] "Should make people with hope ...not let people fear";[33] "(if the official) get angry constantly, people would leave far away";[34] "to judge/to inspect wisely and knowing the capacity of people, to be good at estimating the capacity of people."[35]

We could find so many examples in *the Way to Be a Good Official*, leading the officials to be kind to his people. And this was a rather good demand for officials to obtain as an ethical need.

From this part, we could see that the ethics for an official was high and the boundary for what to do and what not to do was clear through the bamboo

---

31 The organization team of bamboo slips of Qin tomb of Shuihudi 睡虎地秦墓竹簡整理小組, *Bamboo slips of Qin tomb of Shuihudi*《睡虎地秦墓竹簡》, Beijing, Cultural Relics Press, 1978. p.281.

32 The organization team of bamboo slips of Qin tomb of Shuihudi 睡虎地秦墓竹簡整理小組, *Bamboo slips of Qin tomb of Shuihudi*《睡虎地秦墓竹簡》, Beijing, Cultural Relics Press, 1978. p.285.

33 The organization team of bamboo slips of Qin tomb of Shuihudi 睡虎地秦墓竹簡整理小組, *Bamboo slips of Qin tomb of Shuihudi*《睡虎地秦墓竹簡》, Beijing, Cultural Relics Press, 1978. p.288.

34 The organization team of bamboo slips of Qin tomb of Shuihudi 睡虎地秦墓竹簡整理小組, *Bamboo slips of Qin tomb of Shuihudi*《睡虎地秦墓竹簡》, Beijing, Cultural Relics Press, 1978. p.288.

35 The organization team of bamboo slips of Qin tomb of Shuihudi 睡虎地秦墓竹簡整理小組, *Bamboo slips of Qin tomb of Shuihudi*《睡虎地秦墓竹簡》, Beijing, Cultural Relics Press, 1978. p.281.

slips of *the Way to Be a Good Official*. On the one hand , it clarified the ethical needs for the officials and official-learn-to-be; on the other hand , this group of ethical teaching material was basically fit in the policy of "law as education" 以法為教 and "officials as teachers" 以吏為師.

7.2. Other 2 different statutes of the state of Wei 魏 in the ethical teaching materials of *the Way to Be a Good Official*

There was an unexpected situation of the ethical teaching materials of *the Way to Be a Good Official*. 2 statutes of Wei state were found rather unexpectedly as an appendix to the collection of *the Way to Be a Good Official*. They were *the Wei Statute on Households*《魏戶律》and *the Wei Statute on Emergency Troops*《魏奔命律》.

In *the Wei Statute on Households*《魏戶律》,[36] the regulation of the household of Wei State was also found in *Qin bamboo slips of Yunmeng Shuihudi*. One possibility was that this regulation was similar or still be used in Qin, so that, it was buried with Xi.

"The 25th year, the intercalary doubled 12th month whose first day was Bing Wu, on the day Xin Hai, announcement to the Chancellor: People sometimes leave the settlements (to go and) dwell in the countryside, intruding among others' orphans and widows and demanding peoples' wives and daughters. This is against the ancient traditions of the state. From now on, …, inn-keepers, debt salves and stepfather must not be made to form household and must not be given, make them serve, but still note in their register:

---

36 Theorganization team of bamboo slips of Qin tomb of Shuihudi 睡虎地秦墓竹簡整理小組, *Bamboo slips of Qin tomb of Shuihudi*《睡虎地秦墓竹簡》, Beijing, Cultural Relics Press, 1978. pp.292-293.

'Formerly debt-slave X of X Village, the old man's great-grandson'."[37]

Except for*the Wei Statute on Households* 《魏戶律》, there was another regulation of Wei was buried in the tomb of Xi in Yungmeng Shuihudi. And it was titled as *the Wei Statute on Emergency Troops* 《魏奔命律》.[38]

"The 25th year, the intercalary doubled 12th month whose first day was Bing Wu, on the day Xin Hai, an announcement to the Chancellor: ..., innkeepers, debt-slaves, and stepfather sometimes induce people not to work and not to take care of their houses. The Solitary Men do not wish this. In case they were killed, I cannot bear this (for the sake of) their clansmen. Now dispatch them to join the army. The generals must not show pity. When beef is prepared to feed the troops, grant them one third (of a peck) of boiled grain, but do not give them meat. When attacking walled towns, use them when there is an insufficiency; let the generals use them to fill the moats."[39]

As far as the author concerned, these 2 statutes might be written in the collection because they meet the needs of the ethical requirement for the officials of Qin, and some scholars[40] seconded with their research and

---

37 A.F.P. Huleswe, *Remnants of Ch'in Law: An Annotated Translation of the Ch'in Legal and Administrative Rules of the 3rd Century B.C. Discovered in Yun-meng Prefecture*, Hu-pei Province, in 1975, Leiden, E. J. Brill Publisher, 1985.p.208.

38 Theorganization team of bamboo slips of Qin tomb of Shuihudi 睡虎地秦墓竹簡整理小組, *Bamboo slips of Qin tomb of Shuihudi* 《睡虎地秦墓竹簡》, Beijing, Cultural Relics Press, 1978. p.294.

39 A.F.P. Huleswe, *Remnants of Ch'in Law: An Annotated Translation of the Ch'in Legal and Administrative Rules of the 3rd Century B.C. Discovered in Yun-meng Prefecture*, Hu-pei Province, in 1975, Leiden, E. J. Brill Publisher, 1985.pp.209-210.

40 Theorganization team of bamboo slips of Qin tomb of Shuihudi 睡虎地秦墓竹簡整理小組, *Bamboo slips of Qin tomb of Shuihudi* 《睡虎地秦墓竹簡》, Beijing, Cultural Relics Press, 1978. p.281.

admitted *the Wei Statute on Households*《魏戶律》and *the Wei Statute on Emergency Troops*《魏奔命律》might not be randomly picked in the collection but rather precious documents of *the Way to Be a Good Official.*

Chapter Eight
Conclusion

Looking back at this thesis with some historical-educational perspectives, we realize that a group of teaching materials of Pre-Qin was certainly taught. The content of the teaching materials of Pre-Han was varied in terms of   legal documents, literacy, mathematics and ethical documents, and so on.

In Qin China, Legalist school played a key role in educational policies making, determining   who to learn, what to learn, and how to learn.   Such as Shang Yang, his policy "Burning the *Shi*《詩》and the *Shu*《書》to clarify the Law" made the foundation that the teaching material was changed for the classic documents from legal materials. The basic tone of the education system of Pre-Han changed into learning Law as the propriety educational target. And such as Li Si, according to the handed-down documents, he did not concern much about education; however, he also influenced the education system tremendously with the policy: Officials as teachers. This legalist's thought directly resulted in that except the original duty and responsibility, officials had an extra work as teachers, teaching the people the knowledge of legislation so that the people knew what to do and what not to do. Those educational policies made by the leading thought of Legalist's school made   a huge impact on the education system in ancient China.

Based on the newly excavateddocumentof Bamboo Slips of Qin Tomb of Shuihudi, the legal teaching material is a systematic group of legislative documents. It gathers so many contents covering many aspects of society. They are both laws and legal teaching materials at the same time based on the policy

"Law as education" of Legalist's school. With the biggest proportion, is *the Eighteen Qin Statutes*, it includes 18 different groups of regulations in theaspectof Agriculture, Stables, and Parks, Granaries, Currency, Passes and Markets, Artisans, Norms for Artisans, Equalizing Artisans, Labor, Controller of works, Establishment of officials, Checking, Aristocratic rank bestowed for military action, Rations for holders of passports, Forwarding of documents, Minister of finance and miscellaneous, Commandant and miscellaneous and Dependent states. Exceptfor *the Eighteen Qin Statutes*, the other 4 groups related to legal teaching materials were unearthed as well, including *the statutes concerning Checking, Miscellaneous Excerpts from Qin Statutes, Answers to Questions Concerning Qin Statutes* and *Models for Sealing and Investigating*. Since the main content of *the statutes concerning Checking* is overlapped with *the Statutes concerning Checking of the Eighteen Qin Statutes*, the thesis does not further elaborate it. All the legal teaching materials found in the newly excavated document of *the Eighteen Qin Statutes* were analyzed about their meanings part by part. Through the analysis, we were surprised by the abundant, commodity, and rich details of the legal teaching material of pre-Han China.

After the discussion of the legal teaching material of pre-Han China, itintrigued other academic problems about the education of pre-Han China. What were the literacy levels of the people during that time? If you want to teach the people of the law based on the policy "Law as education", you had at least acknowledged a certain amount of literacy so that you could achieve the goal. So, using the newly excavated document of *the Han Bamboo Slips of Zhang Jia Shan* and*the chapter of Cang Jie of*the *Han bamboo slip of Beijing University*, the following chapter talked about the literary situation of pre-Han China. And we found it at least matches the result from the handed-down document of *Han Shu* "People of Qin had to literate 9000 characters to become an official". Furthermore, the literacy education of officials might be higher than just 9000 characters according to the discussion of the analysis.

Except for learning and understanding the law for not violating the law, people also had to be educated with so mathematician knowledge to tackle their daily problems. In the chapter of teaching materials of mathematics, mathematics education of pre-Han China was divided into land and taxation problems, storage and goods problem, and labor and manufacture industry problem to discussed. Every problem has its cases written in the newly excavated document. In the meanwhile, we find the mathematician education of pre-Han was quite systematic and covered almost all the society, which means the teaching materials of mathematics level was adequately high in pre-Han China.

As for *The Way to Be a Good Official* in pre-Han China, it was more like anethics guide for the officials. Due to it was anethics guide, it must be something that officials had to learn about, that, made it undouble a teaching material. Even though   it was found in the same place as Shuihudi with other legal teaching materials, we made it separated as a chapter, because it is not a legal document. This newly excavated document has its characteristic of contents.

The newly excavated document gives great help for us to understand the teaching materials of the legalist's school in pre-Han China; however, many problems remain unsolved. Did they have a guideline for education for different social classes? Did the lawfully implement by "officials as teachers" or by legal practice or by both? What was the weight of them? Did the officials have unified examinations for the understanding of *"The Way to Be a Good Official"* in the education system? Let's look forward to more newly excavated documents to be found and unearthed, so that more influential historical education problems could be coped with and could give us a clearer answer of the whole picture during that time.

Bibliography

〔Han〕Ban Gu〔漢〕班固, *Han Shu/History of the Former Han.* Shanghai: Shanghai Guji Press, 2003.

〔Han〕Dong Zhongshu〔漢〕董仲舒 attributed, eds. Su Yu 蘇輿. *Luxuriant Dew on Spring and Autumn* 《春秋繁露》. Beijing: Zhonghua Press. 1992.

〔Han〕Han Ying〔漢〕韓嬰 Attributed, *Han Ying's Illustration of the Didactic Application of the Book of Odes*《韓詩外傳》.Shanghai: Shanghai Shangwu Yinshuguan.1925

〔Han〕Shi You〔漢〕史遊, *Ji Jiu*《急就篇》. Changsha: Yuelu College Press, 1989.

〔Han〕Sima Qian〔漢〕司馬遷, *Shi Ji/Records of the History.* Xuchang: Zhongzhou Guji Press, 1996.

〔Han〕Sima Qian〔漢〕司馬遷. annotated. Pei Yin, Sima Zhen, and Zhang Shoujie. *Records of the Grand Historian*《史記》. Beijing: Zhonghua Press. 1959.

〔Han〕Sima Qian〔漢〕司馬遷. trans.Yang Xianyi and Gladys Yang *Selections Form Records of the Historian.* Beijing: Foreign Languages Press, 2001.

〔Warring States〕Han Fei〔戰國〕韓非, trans. W.K.Liao, and translated into modern Chinese by Zhang Jue 張覺. *Han Fei Zi.* Beijing: The Commercial Press, 2015.

〔Warring States〕Shang Yang〔戰國〕商鞅, trans. Duyvendak J. J. L., Gao Heng. *The Book of Lord Shang.* Beijing: The Commercial Press, 2006.

〔Yuan〕Ma Duanlin〔元〕馬端臨,*Wen Xian Tong Kao.* Beijing: Zhonghua Book Company, 1986.

Adler, Philip J., and Randall L. Pouwels. *World Civilizations.* Wadsworth: Cengage Learning, 2012.

Allan, Sarah. *Buried Ideas: Legends of Abdication and Ideal Government in Early Chinese Bamboo-Slip Manuscripts.* New York: State University of New York Press, 2015.

Ames, Roger T. *The Art of Rulership: A Study in Ancient Chinese Political Thought.* Honolulu, University of Hawaii Press, 1983.

An, Zuozhang 安作璋, and Xiong Tieji 熊鐵基.*Qin Han guanzhi shigao/The bureaucratic system of the Qin and Han dynasties*《秦漢官制史稿》. Jinan: Qilu Shushe. 1984.

Anderson, Rufus. *History of the Missions of The American Board of Commissioners for Foreign Missions to the Oriental Churches, Volume I.* New York: Valde Books, 2009.

Anderson, Rufus. *History of the Missions of the American Board of Commissioners for Foreign Missions to the Oriental Churches, Volume II.* New York: Valde Books, 2009.

Ariel, Yoav. *K'ung-Ts'ung-Tzu The K'ung Family Masters' Anthology.* Princeton, N.J.: Princeton University Press, 1989.

Bai Shouyi 白壽彝, Gao Min 高敏, and An Zuozhang 安作璋, eds. *Zhongguo tongshi: Qin-Han shiqi volume 5/A general history of China: Qin-Han period, vol:5*《中國通史：秦漢時期（第五卷）》. Shanghai: Shanghai Renmin Press. 1995.

Bai Shuoyi 白壽彝. *An Outline History of China.* Beijing: Foreign Languages Press, 2008.

Bai Xi 白奚. *Jixiaxue yanjiu: Zhongguo gudai de sixiang ziyou he baijia zhengming/A study of Jixiaxue: freedoms and debates of ancient Chinaphilosophers*《稷下學研究：中國古代的思想自由與百家爭鳴》. Beijing: Sanlian Shudian. 1998.

Bai Yulan 白于藍, Reading Notes on the text "Wei Li Zhi Dao "of the Shuihudi Qin Dynasty Bamboo Strip Manuscripts 睡虎地秦簡《為吏之道》校讀劄記. *Jianghan Archaeology* 《江漢考古》, 2010: 125-131.

Balazs, Étienne, trans. H. M. Wright, ed. Arthur F. Wright. *Chinese civilization and bureaucracy: Variations on a theme.* New Haven and London: Yale Univ. Press. 1964.

Balazs, Étienne, trans. H. M. Wright, ed. Arthur F. Wright.*Chinese civilization and bureaucracy: Variations on a theme.* New Haven and London: Yale Univ. Press. 1964.

Bernard, Noel. *Studies on the Ch'u Silk Manuscript. Part 1: Scientific Examination of an Ancient Chinese Document as a Prelude to Decipherment, Translation, and Historical Assessment. Part 2: Translation and Commentary.* Canberra: Australian National University, 1972, 1973.

Bielenstein, Hans. *The bureaucracy of Han times.* Cambridge: Cambridge Univ. Press. 1980.

Bloodworth, *Ching, and Dennis Bloodworth. The Chinese Machiavelli.* New Jersey: Transaction Publishers, 2004.

Bodde, Derk. *China's First Unifier. Leiden: Brill. 1938; rpt.,* Hong Kong: Hong Kong University Press, 1967.

Boltz, William G. *The Origin and Early Development of the Chinese Writing System, American Oriental Series, vol. 78.* New Haven, Conn.: American Oriental Society, 1994.

Bu Xianqun 卜憲群. *Qin Han guanliao zhidu/ Qin-Han bureaucratic system* 《秦漢官僚制度》. Beijing: Shehui Kexue Wenxian Press.2002.

Can Xiao 蕭燦, *The research of Mathematics of Qin bamboo slips collected by Yulu College.* Beijing: Social Sciences Academic Press, 2015.

Cao Lvning 曹旅寧, *New discovery of Qin Law* 《秦律新探》. Beijing: China Social Sciences Press, 2002.

Cao Lvning 曹旅寧, Problems of the Statute Title of the Major of Official Carriages of Strips of Shuihudi of Qin 睡虎地秦簡《公車司馬獵律》的律名問題. *Archaeology* 《考古》, 2011: 78-80.

Cellen, Christopher. The Suàn shù shu̅筭數書, Writings on reckoning: Rewriting the history of early Chinese mathematics in the light of an excavated manuscript. *Historia Mathematica*, 2007: 10-44.

Ch'ien Mu 錢穆. *Ch'in Han shih*《秦漢史》. Hong Kong: Hsin Hua yin-shua Ku-fen Kung-ssu, 1957.

Ch'ien Mu 錢穆. *Liang Han ching-hsüeh chin-ku-wen p'ing-i*《兩漢經學今古文平議》. Hong Kong: Hsin-ya Yen-chiu-so, 1958.

Ch'ü T'ung-Tsu 瞿同祖.2003. *Zhongguo fengjian shehui/ China's feudal society*《中國封建社會》. Shanghai: Shanghai Renmin Press.

Ch'ü T'ung-Tsu 瞿同祖. *Law and Society in Traditional China.* Beijing: The Commercial Press, 2011.

Chan, Wing-tsit 陳榮捷. *A Source Book in Chinese Philosophy.* Princeton, N.J.: Princeton University Press, 1963.

Chang, Chun-Shu. *The Rise of the Chinese Empire: Nation, State, and Imperialism in Early China ca. 1600 B.C.-A.D. 8, vol. 1.* MI: University of Michigan Press. 2007.

Chen Enlin 陳恩林. 1991. *Xian Qin junshi zhidu yanjiu/A study of the early*

China military institutions《先秦軍事制度研究》. Changchun: Jilin Wenshi Press.

Chen Jingpan 陳景磐. *Confucius as a Teacher.* Beijing: Foreign Languages Press, 1990.

Chen Mengjia 陳夢家. Yinxu buci zongbu 《殷墟卜辭綜述》. Beijing: Kexue, 1956.

Chen Mengjia 陳夢家, *An Introduction to Chinese Paleography* 《中國文字學》. Beijing: Zhonghua Book Company, 2006.

Chen Ping 陳平. *Guan Long wenhua yu Ying Qin wenming/The Guan Long culture and Ying Qin civilization*《關隴文化與嬴秦文明》. Nanjing: Jiangsu Jiaoyu Press.2005.

ChenQitian 陳啟天,*Introduction of Chinese Legalism*《中國法家概論》. Beijing: Zhonghua Book Company, 1936.

Chen Qiyou 陳奇猷. *Lü Shi Chunqiu jiaoshi*《呂氏春秋校釋》. 2 vols. Shanghai: Xuelin. 1984; rpt., Taipei: Huazheng, 1988.

Chen Rui 陳銳, and Gao Yuan 高袁. A Kind of Simple Technique: Legal Interpretation Method inthe Asks and Answers to Law Written in the Bamboo Slips Found in the Qin Dynasty Tomb 樸素的技巧:《法律問答》中的法律解釋方法. *Zheng Fa Lun Cong*《政法論叢》, 2011: 60-65.

Chen Songchang etc. 陳松長等, *The Compilation, and Research of the Qin Bamboo Slips of Academy of Yuelu* 《嶽麓書院藏秦簡的整理與研究》. Shanghai: East-west Book Co., 2014.

Chen Songchang 陳松長 and Liao Mingchun 廖明春. Boshu Ersanzi wen, yi zhi yi, Yao shiwen 帛書二三子問易之義要釋文. *Daojia wenhua yanjiu*《道家文化研究》1993(3):424-35.

Chen Songchang 陳松長, A Summarize of the Qin Slips Collected by Yuelu Academy 嶽麓書院所藏秦簡綜述. *Wenwu*, 2009: 75-88.

Chen Wei 陳偉, *The First Exploration of Chu Bamboo Slips of Baoshan* 《包山楚簡初探》. Wuhan: Wuhan University Press, 1996.

Chen Wei 陳偉, *Liye Qin bamboo slips An annotated explanation* 《里耶秦簡牘校釋》. Wuhan: Wuhan University Press, 2012.

Chen Wei 陳偉, *The Proofread, and Citation of the Qin Bamboo Slips of Liye* 《里耶秦簡牘校釋》. Wuhan: Wuhan University Press, 2012.

Chen Wei 陳偉. 1996. *Baoshan Chujian chutan/A study of Baoshan Chujian* 《包山楚簡初探》. Wuhan: Wuhan Daxue Press.

Chen Wutong 陳梧桐, Li Delong 李德龍, eds.Liu Shuguang 劉曙光, *Zhongguo junshi tongshi diwujuan: Xi Han junshi/A military history of China, vol.5: the Western Han Era* 《中國軍事通史第五卷：西漢軍事史》. Beijing: Junshi Kexue Press. 1998.

Chen Zhanfeng 陳戰峰, The Development of Qin Thought and Culture Reflected by Shuihudi Qin Bamboo Slips The Way To Be An Official (Li) 從睡虎地秦簡《為吏之道》看秦思想文化的發展. *Journal of Xidian University (Social Science Edition)* 《西安電子科技大學學報》, 2004: 65-68.

Cheung Wai Po 張偉保, and Wen Rujia 溫如嘉. Early Development of Prefecture and county System: taking Wei State as Centrality 《郡縣制的早期發展：以魏國為中心》.Conference ：the Memorial centenarian of Mr. Yan Gengwang 嚴耕望先生百齡紀念學術研討會. Hong Kong: Hong Kong University, 2016.

Cohen, Jerome A., R. Randle Edwards, eds. Fu-mei Chang Chen, *Essays on China's legal tradition*. Princeton: Princeton Univ. Press, 1980.

Cotterell, Arthur. *The First Emperor of China*. New York: Holt, Rinehart, and Winston, 1981.

Creel, Herrlee G. Shen Pu-Hai: *A Chinese Political Philosopher of the Fourth Century B.C.* Chicago: University of Chicago Press, 1974.

Creel, Herrlee G. *What Is Taoism?* Chicago: University of Chicago Press, 1970.

Creel, Herrlee Glessner. *The Birth of China: A Study of the Formative Period of Chinese Civilization.* New York Reynal & Hitchcock, 1937; 6th printing, New York: Ungar, 1967.

Crump, J. I. *Chan-Kuo Ts'e*《戰國策》.Ann Arbor: Center for Chinese Studies: the University of Michigan, 1996.

Davis, J. Francis. *China During the War and Since The Peace.* Montana: Kessinger Publishing, LLC, 2009.

Dawson, Raymond. *The Chinese Experience.* New Haven: Phoenix Press, 2000; rpt. 2005.

De Bary, William Theodore et al. *Sources of Chinese Tradition.* New York: Columbia University Press, 1999.

Denecke, Wiebke. *The Dynamics of Masters Literature: Early Chinese Thought from Confucius to Han Feizi.* Cambridge: Harvard University Asia Center for the Harvard-Yenching Institute, 2010.

Denis, Twitchett, and Michael Loewe. *The Cambridge History of China. Cambridge*, UK: Cambridge University Press, 1986.

Di Cosmo, Nicola. *Ancient China and Its Enemies.* Cambridge, UK: Cambridge University Press, 2002; rpt. 2010.

Dong Yue 董說. *Qi guo kao*《七國考》. Beijing: Chung Wah Book Company, 1956.

Du Zhengsheng 杜正勝. *Bian hu qi min: Chuantong zhengzhi shehui jiegou zhi xingcheng*《編戶齊民：傳統政治社會結構之行成》. Taipei: Lianjing. 1991.

Du Zhengsheng 杜正勝. *Gudai shehui yu guojia/Society and state in the ancient world*《古代社會與國家》. Taibei: Yunchen Wenhua Shiye Gufen Youxian Gongsi. 1992.

Du Zhengsheng 杜正勝. *Zhou dai chengbang*《周代城邦》. Taipei: Lianjing. 1979.

Dubs, Homer H. *The Works of Hsuntze: Translated from the Chinese with Notes*. London: Arthur Probsthain, 1928.

Duyvendak J. J. L., trans. Gao. Heng., Trans. *The Book of Lord Shang*. Guilin: Guangxi Normal University Press, 2006.

Ebrey, Patricia Buckley. *Chinese Civilization*. New York: Free Press, 1993.

Elman, Benjamin A and Martin Kern. *Statecraft and Classical Learning*. Leiden: Brill, 2010.

Eric L Hutton. *Xunzi*. Princeton: Princeton University Press, 2014.

Fairbank, John King. *China A New History*. Cambridge, Mass.: Belknap Press of Harvard University Press, 2006.

Falkenhausen, Lothar von. *Chinese Society in the Age of Confucius (1000-250 BC)*. Los Angeles: Cotsen Institute of Archaeology, University of California, 2006.

Fischer, Paul. *Shizi: China's First Syncretist*. New York: Columbia University Press, 2012.

Fu Juyou 傅舉有 and Chen Songchang 陳松長. *Mawangdui Han mu wenwu*《馬王堆漢墓文物》. Changsha: Hunan, 1992.

Fu Zhengyuan. *China's Legalists the Earliest Totalitarians and Their Art of Ruling*. New York: M.E. Sharpe, 1996.

Fung, Yu-lan 馮友蘭, Derk Bodde. *A History of Chinese Philosophy*. Princeton: Princeton University Press, 1952.

Fung, Yu-lan 馮友蘭, Derk Bodde. *A Short History of Chinese Philosophy*. New York: Free Press, 1948; rpt. 1976.

Fung, Yu-lan 馮友蘭. trans. Zhao, Fusan. *A Short Histroy of Chinese Philosophy (English-Chinese Version)*. Tianjin: Tianjin Social Sciences Academic Press, 2007.

Gao Heng 高亨, *Transliteration of Book of Shang Yang*《商君書註譯》. Beijing: Qinghua University Press, 2011.

Gen, Liang. *A Forgotten Book Chun Qiu Guliang Zhuan*. Singapore: Global Publishing, 2011.

Granet, Marcel. *Chinese Civilization*. Cleveland, OH: Meridian Books. 1964.

Greel, Herrlee G. *The Origins of Statecraft in China : The Western Chou Empire*. Chicago: University of Chicage Press, 1970.

Gu Derong 顧德融, and Zhu Shunlong 朱順龍. *Chunqiu shi/History of the spring and autumn period*《春秋史》. Shanghai: Shanghai Renmin Press. 2001.

GuShikao 顧史考, *The Macro and Micro of Qin's Confucianism of Chu Bamboo Slips of Guodian* 《郭店楚簡先秦儒學宏微觀》. Shanghai: Shanghai Guji Press, 2012.

Guanzi 管子全譯. *Annotated and translated by Xie Haofan and Zhu Yingpin*. Guizhou: Guizhou Renmin Press. 1990.

Guo Moruo 郭沫若. *Liang Zhou jinwenci daxi tulu kaoshi*《兩周金文辭大系圖錄考釋》. Beijing: Kexue, 1958.

Guo Moruo 郭沫若. *Qingtong shidai*《青銅時代》. Shanghai: Qunyi, 1946.

Guo Qijia 郭齊家. *A History of Chinese Educational Thought*. Beijing: Foreign Languages Press, 2009.

Guo Shangxing et al. *A History of Chinese Culture*. Kaifeng Shi: Henan University Press, 1993.

Guo Shuchun 郭書春, *Translation and Annotation of Jiuzhang Suanshu or the Nine Chatpters on Mathematical Procedures*《九章算術譯註》. Shanghai: Shanghai Guji Press, 2009.

Guo, Keyu 郭克煜. *Luguoshi/History of Lu*《魯國史》. Beijing: Renmin Press. 1994.

Han Fei and Burton Watson. *Han Fei Tzu*. New York: Columbia University Press, 1964.

Han Wei 韓巍, The mathematical resources of Qin bamboo slips collected by Peking University 北大秦簡中的數學文獻. *Wenwu*, 2012: 85-89.

Han Xing 韓星. *Ru Fa zhenghe: Qin Han zhengzhi wenhua lun/Integration of Confucionism and Legalism: Qin-Han political culture*《儒法整合：秦漢政治文化論》. Beijing: Zhongguo Shehui Kexue Press. 2005.

Harry Miller. *The Gongyang Commentary on the Spring and Autumn Annals*《公羊傳》. New York: Palgrave Macmillan, 2015.

He Huaihong 何懷宏. *Shixi shehui jiqi jieti: Zhongguo lishi shang de Chunqiu shidai/ The hereditary society and its collapse: the Spring and Autumn Period in Chinese history*《世襲社會及其解體：中國歷史上的春秋時代》. Beijing: Sanlian Shudian. 1996.

He Runkun 何潤坤. Lun Qin wangchao de falü sixiang/On Qin's legal thought 論秦王朝的法律思想. *Qin wenhua luncong* . Xi'an: Xibei Daxue Press.2003(10):23-36.

He Shuagnjin 何雙金. Tianshui Fangmatan Qin jian zhongshu 天水放馬灘秦簡綜述. *Wenwu,* 1989(2): 23-31.

He Shuagnjin 何雙金. Tianshui Fangmatan Qin mu chutu ditu chutan 天水放馬灘秦墓出土地圖初探. *Wenwu*, 1989(2): 12-22.

He Yuhua 何餘華, Reading Han Scripts　of Peking University of *Cang*　1北
　　大藏漢簡《倉頡篇》研讀剳記（一）, JinboWang 簡帛網,
　　04/12/2015, http://www.bsm.org.cn/show_article.php?id=2391

He Ziquan 何茲全. *Zhongguo gudai shehui/Ancient Chinese Society*《中國古
　　代社會》. Beijing: Beijing Shifan Daxue Press. 2001.

Hou Wailu 侯外盧. *Hou Wailu gudai shehui shilun/Houwailu's writings on
　　ancient China* 《侯外盧古代社會史論》. Shijiazhuang: Hebei
　　Jiaoyu Press. 2003.

Hsing, I-tien and Liu, Tseng-kuei. *Commoners in Ancient China.* Taipei:
　　Academia Sinica, 2013.

Hsu Cho-yun and Katheryn M Linduff. *Western Chou Civilization.* New Haven:
　　Yale University Press, 1988.

Hsu Cho-yun. *A New Cultural History China.* N.Y.: Columbia University Press,
　　1983; rpt. 2006.

Hsu Cho-yun. *Ancient China in Transition.* Stanford, Calif.: Stanford University
　　Press, 1965.

Hsu Cho-yun. *History of the Western Zhou*《西周史》. Beijing: Sanlian
　　Shudian. 1994.

Hsü Fu-guan 徐復觀. *Liang Han ssu-hsiang shih* 《兩漢思想史》. Taipei:
　　T'ai-wan Hsüeh- sheng Shu-chü, 1976.

Hsü T'ien-lin 徐天麟. *His-Han hui-yao* 《西漢會要》. 2 vols. Shanghai: Jen-
　　min Ch'u-pan-she, 1976.

http://www.gwz.fudan.edu.cn/Web/Show/2717

Hu Liuyuan and Feng Zhuohui. *Legal Systems of Xia, Shang and Western Zhou:
　　A History.* Beijing: The Commercial Press, 2009.

Hu Pingsheng 胡平生, After　Reading *Cang*　11 讀《蒼》剳記十一, The

research center of the newly excavated document of Fudan 復旦大學出土文獻與古文字研究中心, 15/01/2016, http://www.gwz.fudan.edu.cn/Web/Show/2727

Hu Pingsheng 胡平生, After Reading *Cang* 12 讀《蒼》劄記十二, The research center of the newly excavated document of Fudan 復旦大學出土文獻與古文字研究中心, 20/01/2016, http://www.gwz.fudan.edu.cn/Web/Show/2735

Hu Pingsheng 胡平生, After Reading *Cang* 10 讀《蒼》劄記十, The research center of the newly excavated document of Fudan 復旦大學出土文獻與古文字研究中心, 10/01/2016, http://www.gwz.fudan.edu.cn/Web/Show/2722

Hu Pingsheng 胡平生, After Reading *Cang* 4 讀《蒼》劄記四, The research center of the newly excavated document of Fudan 復旦大學出土文獻與古文字研究中心, 30/12/2015, http://www.gwz.fudan.edu.cn/Web/Show/2704

Hu Pingsheng 胡平生, After Reading *Cang* 5 讀《蒼》劄記五, The research center of the newly excavated document of Fudan 復旦大學出土文獻與古文字研究中心, 31/12/2015, http://www.gwz.fudan.edu.cn/Web/Show/2706

Hu Pingsheng 胡平生, After Reading *Cang* 7 讀《蒼》劄記七, The research center of the newly excavated document of Fudan 復旦大學出土文獻與古文字研究中心, 04/01/2016, http://www.gwz.fudan.edu.cn/Web/Show/2714

Hu Pingsheng 胡平生, After Reading *Cang* 8 讀《蒼》劄記八, The research center of the newly excavated document of Fudan 復旦大學出土文獻與古文字研究中心, 08/01/2016,

Hu Pingsheng 胡平生, After Reading *Cang* 9 讀《蒼》劄記九, The research center of the newly excavated document of Fudan 復旦大學出土文獻與古文字研究中心, 09/01/2016, http://www.gwz.fudan.edu.cn/Web/Show/2721

Hu Pingsheng 胡平生, After Reading *Cang* 3 讀《蒼》劄記三, The research center of the newly excavated document of Fudan 復旦大學出土文獻與古文字研究中心, 23/12/2015, http://www.gwz.fudan.edu.cn/Web/Show/2693

Hu Pingsheng 胡平生, After Reading *Cang* 6 讀《蒼》劄記六, The research center of the newly excavated document of Fudan 復旦大學出土文獻與古文字研究中心, 02/01/2016,http://www.gwz.fudan.edu.cn/Web/Show/2712

Hu Pingsheng 胡平生, After Reading *Cang* 2 讀《蒼》劄記二, The research center of the newly excavated document of Fudan 復旦大學出土文獻與古文字研究中心, 22/12/2015, http://www.gwz.fudan.edu.cn/Web/Show/2692

Hu Pingsheng 胡平生, After Reading *Cang* 1 讀《蒼》劄記一, The research center of the newly excavated document of Fudan 復旦大學出土文獻與古文字研究中心, 21/12/2015, http://www.gwz.fudan.edu.cn/Web/Show/2687

Hu Pu'an 胡樸安, *Elementary Knowledge of Philology*《文字學常識》. Beijing: Zhonghua Book Company, 2010.

Huang Liuzhu 黃留珠. *Zhongguo gudai xuanguan zhidu shulue/A brief history of the official recruitment system in ancient China*《中國古代選官制度述略》. Xi'an: Shaanxi Renming Press.1989.

Huang Liuzhu 黃留珠, Interpretation of the Statutes on Hardship of strips of

Qin 秦簡《中勞律》釋義 . *Relics and Museology*《文博》, 1997: 65-70.

Huang Liuzhu 黃留珠, Shi Zi, Study Room and Xi Yu Shi: Reading Note of Qin bamboo slips of Yunmeng Shuihudi "史子", "學室"與"喜揄史"——讀雲夢秦簡劄記. *The Journal of Humanities (Bimonthly)*《人文雜志》, 1983.

Huang Zhongye 黃中業. *Zhanguo shengshi/Warring states: a golden age*《戰國盛世》. Kaifeng: Henan Renming Press. 1998.

Hucker, Charles O. *China's Imperial Past: An Introduction to Chinese History and Culture*.Redwood City: Stanford University Press. 1975.

Hui, Victoria Tin-bor. *War and State Formation in Ancient China and Early Modern Europe*. Cambridge: Cambridge University Press. 2005.

Huleswe, A.F.P. *Remnants of Ch'in Law: An Annotated Translation of the Ch'in Legal and Administrative Rules of the 3rd Century B.C. Discovered in Yun-meng Prefecture, Hu-pei Province, in 1975*. Leiden: E. J. Brill Publisher, 1985.

Hulsewé, A. F. P. ed. S. R. Schram.*The influence of the state of Qin on the economy as reflected in the texts discovered in Yunmeng Perfecturein the scope of state power in China,* London: School of Oriental and African Studies; Hong Kong: Press of Chinese Univ., 1985.

Hulsewé, A. F. P. ed. W. L. Idema. *The Legalists and the laws of Ch'in."* In *Leyden studies in Sinology*, Leiden: E. J. Brill, 1981.

Institute for Chinese Ancient Legal Document of China University of Political Science and Law 中國政法大學法律古籍整理研究所, *Translation and Annotation of Criminal Laws in Generations of China*《中國歷代刑法志註譯》. Changchun: Jilin Renmin Press, 1994.

Itô Michiharu 伊藤道治. *Chûgoku Kodai kokka no shibai kôzô* 《中國古代國家の支配構造》. Tokyo: Chuô kôronsha, 1987.

Itô Michiharu 伊藤道治. *Chûgoku Kodai ôcho no keisei* 《中國古代王朝の形成》. Tokyo: Sôbunsha, 1975.

Jia Yi 賈誼. Annotated by Yan Zhenyi, Zhong Xia.*New Writings*《新書校注》. Beijing: Zhonghua Press. 2000.

Jiangling Study Group of the Jiangling Documents 江陵張家山漢簡整理小組, Transcription of Bamboo Suanshushu or a Book of Arithmetic 江陵張家山竹簡《算數書》釋文. *Wenwu*, 2000: 78-84.

Jin Chunfeng 金春峰. *Handai sixiangshi /The history of thought in the Han dynasty*《漢代思想史》. Beijing: Zhongguo Shehui Kexue Press. 1997.

Jin Jingfang 金景芳. *Zhongguo nuli shehui shi/The history of Chinese slavery society* 《中國奴隸社會史》. Shanghai: Shanghai Renmin Press. 1983.

Ju Huanwen 鞠煥文, Reading Han Scripts of Peking University of *Cang* 1北大《倉頡篇》讀書劄記（一）,inboWang 簡帛網, 25/11/2015, http://www.bsm.org.cn/show_article.php?id=2377

Kalinowski, Marc. Manuscript Culture in Present-day China and Its Significance to the Study of Chirographic Practices and Technical Literature in Late Warring States, Qin, and Han. Inaugural International Conference: New Philology and the study of Early China. Macau, 2016.

Kamada Shigeo 鎌田重雄. *Shin Kan seiji seido no kenkyū*《秦漢政治制度の研究》. Tokyo: Nihon Gakujutsu Shinkōkai, 1962.

Kazuo Miyamoto 宮本一夫, trans. Wu Fei 吳菲. *From mythology to History : the mythical age dynasty of Xia* 《從神話到歷史：神話時代夏王朝》. Guilin: Guangxi Normal University Press, 2014.

Kazuyuki Tsuruma 鶴間和幸, trans. Ma Biao 馬彪, *Legacy of the Emperor: the Empire of Qin and Han* 《始皇帝的遺產：秦漢帝國》, Guilin: Guangxi Normal University Press, 2005.

Keay, John. *China: A History*. New York: Haeper Press, 2008.

Keightley, David N. *Sources of Shang History: The Oracle-Bone Inscriptions of Bronze Age China.* Berkeley: University of California Press, 1978. (2nd printing, with minor revisions, 1985.)

Keightley, ed.David N., *The Origins of Chinese Civilization.* Berkeley: University of California Press, 1983.

Kern, Martin. *Text and Ritual in Early China.* Seattle: University of Washington Press, 2005.

Kern, Martin. *The Stele Inscriptions of Ch'in Shih-huang: Text and Ritual in Early Chinese Imperial Representation.* New Haven, CT: American Oriental Society. 2000.

Knoblock, John H. Xunzi: *A Translation and Study of the Complete Works. 3 vols.* Standard, Calif.: Stanford University Press, 1988-1994.

Koichiro Shibata 稻畑耕一郎. The handed down and excavated documents of Chinese ancient areas 《中國古代領域中的傳世典籍與出土資料》.Conference: Inaugural International Conference: New Philology and the study of Early China. Macau, 2016.

Kramers, R. P. *K'ung Tzu Chia Yü: The school sayings of Confucius.* Leiden: E. J. Brill, 1950.

Ku Chieh-kang 顧頡剛. *Ch'in Han ti fang-shih yü ju-sheng*《秦漢的方士與儒生》. Shanghai: Ch' ün-lien Ch'u-pan-she, 1955.

Ku Chieh-kang. *Shih-lin tsa-shih*《史林雜識》. Beijing: Chung-hua Shu-chü, 1963.

Ku Yen-wu 顧炎武. Jih-chih lu 日知錄. Wan-yu wen-k'u ed.

KunihiroYuasa 湯淺邦弘. *The study of the intellectual history of Chu Bamboo and Qin Bamboo during Warring States*《戰國楚簡與秦簡之思想史研究》. Taipei: Wan Juan Lou 萬卷樓, 2006.

Kuo Mo-jo 郭沫若. *Shih p'i-p'an shu*《十批判書》. Chungking: Ch' ün-pan-she, 1945.

Lao Gan 勞榦. *Gudai Zhongguo de lishi yu wenhua/History and culture of ancient China*《古代中國的歷史與文化》. Beijing: Zhonghua Press. 2006.

Lao Kan 勞榦. *Chü-yen Han-chien k'ao-shih*《居延漢簡考釋》. Academia Sinica, Institute of History and Phiology, Special Publication 40. Taipei, 1960.

Laozi., Guanghu He, and Jiyu Ren. *The Book of Lao Zi.* Beijing: Foreign Languages Press, 1993.

LeeCyrus 李紹崑. *The Complete Works of Motzu in English. Beijing:* The Commercial Press, 2009.

Lei Xueqi 雷學琪. *Zhushu jinian yizheng*《竹書紀年義證》. Taipei: Yiwen, 1977.

Levenson, R. Joseph and Franz Schurmann. *China: An Interpretive History. California,* London: University of California Press, 1969.

Lewis, Mark Edward. *Sanctioned Violence in Early China.* Albany: State University of New York Press, 1999.

Lewis, Mark Edward. *The Early Chinese Empires: Qin and Han.* MA: The Belknap Press, 2007.

Li Chi 李濟. *The Beginnings of Chinese Civilization.* Beijing: Foreign Languages Teaching and Research Press, 2011.

Li Cunshan 李存山, *Acritical Biography if Shang Yang: the reformer of Emperorism of Qin* 《商鞅評傳——為秦開帝業的改革家》. Nanning: Guangxi Education Press, 1997.

Li Feng 李鋒. *Bureaucracy and the State in Early China Coverning the Western Zhou*. Cambridge: Cambridge University Press, rpt. 2013.

Li Feng 李鋒. *Early China: A Society and Cultural History. Cambridge.* Cambridge: Cambridge University Press, 2013.

Li Feng. *Landscape and Power in Early China*. Cambridge: Cambridge University Press. 2006.

Li Jin 栗勁, *The General Theory of Qin Law* 《秦律通論》. Jinan: Shangdong Renmin publisher, 1985.

Li Junming 李均明,*Organization and Analysis of the text of strips of Qin and Han*《秦漢簡牘文書分類輯解》. Beijing: Cultural Relics Press, 2009.

Li Ling 李零. *Notes on reading the Guodian bamboo slips*《郭店楚簡校讀記》. Beijing: Beijing Daxue Press. 2002.

Li Mingxiao 李明曉, The Study of Laws in Bamboo Slips Excavated from Ancient Tombs of *the Qin Dynasty in Shuihudi*《睡虎地秦墓竹簡》法律用語研究 [D], Chongqing, Southwest China Normal University, 04/2003.

Li Ping 李平, An Analysis of the Theoretical Dilemma of the Rule of Law of Qin Dynasty——Focusing on Yu Shu & Wei Li zhi Dao of Shuihudi Qin Bamboo Texts 秦"法治"的理論困境透析——以水壺地秦簡《語書》,《為吏之道》為中心. *Academic Exploration* 《學術探索》, 2010: 28-31.

Li Qintong 李勤通, and Zhou Dongping 周東平. Education System of Official

Carrier in the Regulations and Laws of the Initial Stage of Qin 秦漢初期律令中的史官職業教育體系. *Modern University Education* 《現代大學教育》, 2016: 76-81.

Li Qiqian and Wang Shilun ed. *Collected Date on Confucius'Disciples*. Jinan: Shandong Friendship Press, 1991.

Li Xueqin 李學勤. Qingchuan Haojiaping mudu yanjiu 青川郝家坪木牘研究. *Wenwu* 1982(10): 68-72.

Li Xueqin 李學勤. *The lost texts on bamboo and silk and the history of scholarship*《簡帛佚籍與學術史》. Nanchang: Jiangxi Jiaoyu Press. 2004.

Li Xueqin 李學勤 and Kwang-chih Chang 張光直. *Eastern Zhou and Qin Civilizations*. New Haven: Yale University Press, 1985.

Li Xun 李恂, The Research of "Wei Li Zhi Dao" in Qin Dynasty Depending on the Unearthed Qin Jian 《以出土秦簡看秦代"為吏之道"》[D], Jinzhou, Bohai Uniersity, 2018.

Li Yanong 李亞農. *Xinran Zhai shilunji/ Historical writings at Xinran Studio* 《欣然齋史論集》. Shanghai: Shanghai Renmin Press. 1962.

Li Yujie 李玉潔. The nature of the early Chinese state—state power and absolutism in ancient China《中國早期國家性質──中國古代王權和專制主義研究》. Kaifeng: Henan Daxue Press. 1999.

Li Yujie 李玉潔. *Chuguo shi/The history of Ch*u《楚國史》. Kaifeng: Henan Daxue Press. 2002.

Li Yu-ning, ed. S*hang yang's Reforms and State Control in China*. White Plains, N.Y. Sharpe, 1977.

Li Yu-ning, ed. *The politics of historiography: The First Emperor of China*. White Plains, N. Y. :International Arts and Sciences Press, 1975.

Liang Jing 梁靜, *Study of the unearthed Cangjie*《出土〈倉頡篇〉研究》. Beijing: Science Press, 2015.

Liang Qixiong 梁啟雄. *Hanzi qianjie.*《韓子淺解》. Beijing: Zhonghua, 1960.

Liang Qixiong 梁啟雄. *Xunzi jianshi.* 《荀子簡釋》. Beijing: Guji, 1956.

Liao, W. K. *The Complete Works of Han Fei Tzu, A Classic of Chinese Legalism (Volume 1, 2)*. London: Arthur Probsthain, 1939.

Lin Chin-yen 林清源, "Heading Patterns of the Qin Dynasty Bamboo Slips from Shuihudi 睡虎地秦簡標題格式析論." *Bulletin of Institute of History and Philology* 《歷史語言研究所集刊》, 2002: 790-793.

Lin Jianming 林劍鳴. *Qin Han shi/History of Qin and Han*《秦漢史》. Shanghai: Shanghai Renmin Press.2003.

Lin Jianming 林劍鳴. *Qin shi gao/Draft history of Qin*《秦史稿》. Shanghai: Shanghai Renmin Press.1981.

Lin Shoujin 林壽晉. *Xian Qin kaoguxue*《先秦考古學》. Hong Kong: Chinese University Press, 1991.

LingLi 李零,*The Proofread of Chu Bamboo Slips of Guodian*《郭店楚簡校讀記》. Beijing: China Renmin University Press, 2007.

Liu Hainian 劉海年. *Zhanguo Qiguo falü shiliao de zhongyao faxian/ Important discoveries in warring states Qi legal documents*《戰國齊國法律史料的重要發現》. Faxue yanjiu 1987. 2: 72-82.

Liu Qiyu 劉啟釪. Chonglun Pan Geng qian Yin ji qian Yin de yuanyin 重論盤庚遷殷及遷殷的原因. *Shixue yuekan*《史學月刊》.1990:4 1-5.

Liu Wen-tien 劉文典. *Chuang-tzu pu-cheng*《莊子補正》. Shanghai: Shang-wu Yin-shu-kuan, 1947.

Liu Xiang 劉向. *Gardens of Sayings*《說苑》. Shanghai: Shanghai Shangwu Yinshuguan. 1925.

Liu Xuyi 劉緒貽. *China's Confucian rule: a vested interest group that had prevented social change in China* 《中國的儒學統治：既得利益抵制社會變革的典型事例》. Beijing: Renmin Daxue Press. 2006.

Loewe, Michael. *Crisis and Conflict in Han China*. London: Allen & Unwin, 1974.

Loewe, Michael. *Early Chinese Texts*. Berkeley, Calif.: Soc. for the Study of Early China u.a., 1993.

Loewe, Michael. *Records of Han Administration. 2 vols*. Cambridge: Cambridge University Press, 1967.

Lü Wenyu 呂文郁. *The Fief System in Zhou Dynasty (Enlarged Edition)*. Beijing: Social Sciences Academic Press, 2006.

Luo Genze 羅根澤. *Guanzi tanyuan*《管子探源》. Shanghai: Zhonghua, 1931.

Ma Chengyuan 馬承源, ed. *Shang Zhou qingtongqi mingwen xuan*《商周青銅器銘文選》. Beijing: Wenwu, 1988.

Ma Yong 馬鏞, *Educational History of Chinese Families*《中國家庭教育史》. Changsha: Hunan Education Publishing House, 1997.

Major John S. et al. *The Huainanzi Liu An, King of Huainan*. New York: Columbia University Press, 2010.

Martzloff, Jean-Claude. *A History of Chinese Mathematics*. New York: Springer, 1995.

Ma-wang-tui Han mu po-shu cheng-li Hsiao-tsu 馬王堆漢墓帛書整理小組, ed. *Chan-kuo tsung-heng chia shu*《戰國縱橫家書》. Beijing: Wen-wu Ch'u-pan-she, 1976.

Mei, Ruli, Tan, Foyou and Shi, Kecan ed. *General History of Chinese Education (Pre-Qin) Volume 1 & 2*. Beijing: Beijing Normal University Publishing Group. 2013.

Mei, Ruli, Tan, Foyou and Shi, Kecan ed. *General History of Chinese Education (Qin-Han)*. Beijing: Beijing Normal University Publishing Group. 2013.

Meyer, Dirk. *Philosophy on Bamboo: Text and the Production of Meaning in Early China*. Leiden: Brill, 2012.

Michael Loewe , and Shaughnessy, Edward L. ed., *The Cambridge History of Ancient China*. Cambridge University Press, 1999.

Michiharu Itō 伊藤道治, trans. Jiang Lansheng 江藍生,*The Formation of Ancient Dynasties of China*《中國古代王朝的形成》, Beijing: CHUNG WHA Book Company, 2002.

MinGao 高敏,*The First Exploration of Qin bamboo Slips*《雲夢秦簡初探》. Zhengzhou: Henan Renmin Press, 1979.

Miyazaki Ichisada 宮崎市定, *The Research of the Regulation of Nine Grades of Rank in the Feudal Regimes: the History of Former Imperial Examination*《九品官人法研究：科舉前史》. Beijing:CHUNG WHA Book Company, 2008.

Mo, Di and Ian Johnston. *The Book of Master Mo. London*: Penguin Books, 2013.

Mote, Frederick W. *Intellectual Foundations of China*. New York: Alfred A. Knopf, 1989.

Motoo Kudo 工藤元男, *The Country and Society of Qin from the Qin Scripts of Shuihudi*《睡虎地秦簡所見秦代國家與社會》. Shanghai: Shanghai Guji Press, 2018.

Mozi jian gu 墨子間詁. Annotated by Sun Yirang 孫詒讓. *In Xin bian zhu zi ji chengvol. 6.*《新編諸子集成》, Taipei: Shijie, 1974.

Ni Jinbo 倪晉波,*Unearthed Documents and Literature of Qin*《出土文獻與秦國文學》. Beijing: Cultural Relics Press, 2015.

Nienhauser, William H., Jr., ed., with Tsai-fa Cheng, Zongli Lu, and Robert Reynolds, trans. *The Grand Scribe's Records. Vol. 1: The Basic Annals of Pre-Han China by Ssu-ma Ch'ien.* Bloomington: Indiana University Press, 1994.

Niida Noboru 仁井田陞. *Chūgoku hōseishi kenkyū: Tochihō, torihikihō*《中國法制史研究：土地法，取引法》. Tokyo: Tōkyō Daigaku Shuppan Kai, 1960.

Nishijima Sadao 西島定生. *Chûgoku kodai teikoku no keisei to kôzô: Nijû tô shakusei no kenkyû*《中國古代帝國の形成と構造：二十等爵制の研究》. Tokyo: Tokyo daigaku, 1961.

Nivison, David S. *The Riddle of the Bamboo Annals.* Stanford, Cali.: Private publication, 1995.

Onozawa Seiichi 小野澤精一 et al.,ed. *Ki no shisô: Chûgoku ni okerru shizenkan to ningenkan no tenkai* 氣の思想：中國における自然觀と人間觀の展開. Tokyo: Tôkyô daigaku, 1978.

Peerenboom, R. P. *Law and Morality in Ancient China: The Silk Manuscripts of Huang-Lao (SUNY Series in Chinese Philosophy and Culture).* Albany: State University of New York Press, 1993.

Peng Anyu 彭安玉. *All roads lead to the same destination: paths of reforms during the Spring and Autumn and Warring States ears*《殊途同歸：春秋戰國改革的歷史走向》. Nanjing: Nanjing Daxue Press. 2000.

Peng Hao 彭浩, *An annotated explanation on the Book of Calculation of the Han bamboo slips of Zhangjiashan*《張家山漢簡算數書注釋》. Beijing: Science Press, 2011.

Pines, Yuri, *Gideon Shelach-Lavi, Lothar von Falkenhausen, and Robin D. S Yates, ed. Birth of an Empire. California,* London: University of California Press, 2014.

Pines, Yuri. *Foundations of Confucian Thought: Intellectual Life in the Chunqiu Period, 722-453 B.C.E.* Honolulu: University of Hawaii Press, 2002.

Pines, Yuri. *The Everlasting Empire: The Political Culture of Ancient China and Its Imperial Legacy.* Princeton, NJ: Princeton University Press, 2012.

PuJian 蒲堅,*The Copy of the Legality of Ancient China*《中國古代法制叢抄》. Beijing: Guangming Daily Press, 2001.

Qian Baocong 錢寶琮, *History of Chinese Mathematics* 《中國數學史》. Beijing: Science Press, 1992.

Qian Mu 錢穆. *An outline of Chinese history* 《國史大綱》. Beijing: Beijing Shangwu Yinshuguan. 1994.

Qian Mu 錢穆. *The history of the Qin and Han* 《秦漢史》. Beijing: Sanlian Shudian. 2004.

Qian Mu 錢穆. *Xian Qin zhuzi xinian*《先秦諸子繫年》. 2 vols. Shanghai: Shangwu, 1935; rev. rpt. Hong Kong: Hong Kong University Press, 1956.

Qiao Weiping 喬衛平, and Cheng Peijie 程培傑. *Child Education of Ancient Chian*《中國古代幼兒教育》. Hefei: Anhui Educational Publishing House 安徽教育出版社, 1989.

Qin Hualin 秦樺林, Reading West-Han Scripts of Peking University of *Cang 1北大藏西漢簡《倉頡篇》劄記（一）*, JinboWang 簡帛網, 14/11/2015, http://www.bsm.org.cn/show_article.php?id=2355

Qiu Xigui 裘錫圭 *et al. Chinese Writing.* New Haven: Birdtrack Press, 2000.

Qiu Xigui 裘錫圭, *Essentials of Philology*《文字學概要》. Beijing: The Commercial Press, 2001.

Qiu Xigui 裘錫圭, *Ten Topics of Unearthed Ancient Documents of China*《中國出土古文獻十講》. Shanghai: Fudan University Press, 2004.

Rao Zongyi 饒宗頤 and Zeng Xiantong 曾憲通. *Yunmeng Qin jian rishu yanjiu* 《雲夢秦簡日書研究》. Hong Kong: Chinese University Press, 1982.

Richter, Matthias L. *The Embodied Text: Establishing Textual Identity in Early Chinese Manuscripts*. Leiden: Brill, 2013.

Rickett W.Allyn. *Guan Zi*. Boston: Cheng&Tsui Company, 2001.

Rickett.W. Allyn. *Guanzi (Volume Two)*. Princeton: Princeton University Press, 1998.

Riegel, Jeffrey, and John Knoblock. Lü shi chunqiu: *A New Translation. Stanford*, Cali.: Stanford University Press, 1965.

Rong, Zhaozu 容肇祖. *Legalist thought in Three-Jins*《三晉法家的思想》. Chongqing: Shixue Press.1944.

Roth, Harold D. *The Textual History of the Huai-nan Tzu*. Ann Arbor, Mich.: The Association for Asian Studies, 1992.

Russell, Bertrand. *Wisdom of the West*. Beijing: Culture and Art Publishing House, 2004.

Sanft, Charles. *Communication and Cooperation in Early Imperial China*. New York: Suny Press, 2014.

Sarah A Queen, and John S Major. *Luxuriant Gems of the Spring and Autumn* 《春秋繁露》(Attributed to Dong Zhongshu). New York: Columbia University Press, 2016.

Sawyer, Ralph D and Mei-chu¨n Sawyer. The Seven Military Classics of Ancient China Including the Art of War. Boulder: Westview Press, 1993; rpt. 2007.

Schneider, *Laurance A. Ku Chieh-kang and China's New History*. Berkeley: University of California Press, 1971.

Schwartz, Benjamin I. *The World of Thought in Ancient China.* Cambridge, Mass.: Harvard University Press, 1985.

Scott Cook ed. *The Bamboo Texts of Guodian a study & complete translation I & II*, Ithaca, N.Y.: East Asia Program, Cornell University, 2012.

Scott Cook, ed. *The Bamboo Texts of Guodian a study &complete translation I & II*. Ithaca, N.Y.: East Asia Program, Cornell University, 2012.

Shaughnessy, Edward L. *Before Confucius: Studies in the Creation of the Chinese Classics.* Albany, N.Y.: State University of New York Press, 1997.

Shaughnessy, Edward L. *New Sources of Early Chinese History: An Introduction to the Reading of Inscriptions and Manuscripts.* Berkeley: Institute of East Asian Studies and Society for the Study of Early China, 1997.

Shaughnessy, Edward L. *New Sources of Early Chinese History: An Introduction to the Reading of Inscriptions and Manuscripts.* Shanghai: Zhongxi Press, 2013.

Shaughnessy, Edward L. *Sources of Western Zhou History: Inscribed Bronze Vessels.* Berkeley: University of California Press, 1991.

Shelach-Lavi, Gideon. *The Archaeology of Early China.* New York: Cambridge University Press, 2015.

Shen, Changyun 沈長雲 et al. *History of Zhao*《趙國史稿》. Beijing: Zhonghua Press.2000.

Shi Juehuai. *A Critical Biography of Han Fei.* Nanjing: Nanjing University Press, 2009.

Shi Nianhai 史念海. Heshan ji/Essays on China's geography 《河山集》. Beijing: Sanlian Shudian.1963.

Sima, Qian. *Records Of the Grand Historian: Han Dynasty I. II. Ⅲ*.Hong Kong: Columbia University Press, 1993.

Soothill W. E. *The Analects of Confucius*. California: Stanford University Press, 1942.

Ssu-ch'uan sheng po-wu-kuan 四川博物館, and Ch'ing-ch'uan hsien wen-hua kuan 青川縣文化館. Ch'ing-ch'uan hsien ch'u-t'u Ch'in keng-hsiu t'ien lü mu-tu 青川縣出土秦更修田律木牘. *Wenwu*, 1982(1): 1-13.

Ssu-ma, Ch'ien et al. T*he Grand Scribe's Records (Volumn I. II)*. Bloomington: Indiana University Press, 1994.

Steele, John. *The I-Li or Book of Etiquette and Ceremonial*. London: Bibliolife Press, 2014.

Sun Yirang 孫詒讓. *Zhou li zhengyi 14 vols.*《周禮正義》. Rpt. Beijing: Zhonghua, 1987.

SunKaitai 孫開泰. *A Brief History of Legalism in China*《法家史話》. Taipei: Kuo Chia Publishing Co., 2004.

Taichirō Nishida 西田太一郎, trans. Duan Qiuguan 段秋關. *The Research of Chinese Criminal Law* 《中國刑法史研究》. Beijing: Peking University Press, 1985.

Takezoe, Shin'ichiro. *Zuo Shi Hui Zhan*《左氏會箋》. Chengdu: Bashu Book Press 巴蜀書社, 2008.

Takigawa Kametarō 瀧川龜太郎,*Shiki kaichū kōshō* 《史記會注考證》. 10 vols. Tokyo: Tōhō Bunka Gakuin Tōkyō Kenkyūjo, 1932-34; rpt. Peking: Wen-hsüen Ku-chi K'an-hang she, 1955.

Tan, Qixiang 譚其驤, ed. *Zhongguo lishi dituji, vol.1*《中國歷史地圖集第一冊》. Beijing: Zongguo Ditu Press.1982.

Tang Lan 唐蘭. Huang Di si jing chu tan 黃帝四經初探. *Wenwu* 1974(10): 48-52.

Tang Lan 唐蘭. Mawangdui chutu laozi yi ben juan qian gu yi shu de yanjiu:

Jian lun qi yu Han chu ru fa douzheng de guanxi 馬王堆出土老子乙本卷前古佚書的研究：兼論其與漢初儒法鬥爭的關係. *Kaogu xuebao*《考古學報》 1975(1): 7-38.

Tang Lan 唐蘭, *Introduction of Paleography* 《古文字學導論》. Jina: Shangdong Qilu Press, 1981.

Temple, Robert K. G. *The Genius of China*. Rochester Vermont: Inner Traditions, 2011.

The editing department of CHUNG WHA Book Company, *Research of Qin Bamboo Slip of Yunmeng*《雲夢秦簡研究》. Beijing: CHUNG WHA Book Company, 1981.

The Organization team of bamboo slips of Qin tomb of Shuihudi 睡虎地秦墓竹簡整理小組, *Bamboo slips of Qin tomb of Shuihudi* 《睡虎地秦墓竹簡》. Beijing: Wenwu Press, 1978.

The Organization team of No.247 Tomb of Zhangjiashan 張家山二四七號漢墓之整理小組, *Bamboo Slips of No.247 Tomb of Zhangjiashan*《張家山漢墓竹簡[二四七號墓]》. Beijing: Cultural Relics Press, 2006.

The Peking University Excavated Manuscript Research Center edited 北京大學出土文獻研究所編. *Peking University Bamboo Strips of Xi Han*《北京大學藏西漢竹書》. Shanghai: Shanghai Guji Press, 2015.

Tjan Tjoe Som. Po hu t'ung 白虎通. *The Comprehensive Discussion in the White Tiger Hall. 2 vols*. Leiden: Brill, 1949.

Tong, Shuye 童書業. A study on Zuo's commentary《春秋左傳研究》. Shanghai: Shanghai Renmin Press.1980.

Tsien Tsuen-Hsuin. *Written on Bamboo and Silk: The Beginning of Chinese Books andInscriptions*. Chicago: University of Chicago Press, 1962; rpt. 2004; 2013.

Tsien Tsuen-Hsuin 錢存訓, *Written on Bamboo & Silk, The Beginnings of Chinese Books and Inscriptions, Second Edition*. Chicago: University of Chicago Press, 2004.

Tsinghua University Unearthed Literature Research and Protection Center ed., 清華大學出土文獻研究與保護中心編 and leaded by Li Xueqin 李學勤主編. *Tsinghua University Collection of Warring States Bamboo Slips, Vol. 4* 《清華大學藏戰國竹簡（肆）》. Shanghai: East-west Book Co., 2013.

Tuner, Karen. Rule of Law Ideals in Early China. *Journal of Chinese Law* 1992(6): 1-44.

Tuner, Karen. The Theory of Law in the Ching-fa. *Early China* 1989(14):55-76.

Twitchett, Denis, and Michael Loewe, eds. *The Cambridge History of China. Vol. 1: The Ch'in and Han Empire*. Cambridge University Press, 1986.

Waley, Arthur. *Three Ways of Thought in Ancient China*. California: Stanford University Press, 1939.

Walker, Richard Louis. *The Multi-State System of Ancient China*. Westport. CT: Greenwood Press, 1971.

Wang Changhua 王長華. *Scholars and politic in the Spring and Autumn and Warring States eras*《春秋戰國士人與政治》. Shanghai: Shanghai Renmin Press.1997.

Wang Chong 王充,*Fair Discussions*《論衡全譯》. Guizhou: Guizhou Renmin Press. 1990.

Wang Gesen 王閣森, Tang Zhiqing 唐致卿. *Qi guo shi*《齊國史》. Ji'nan: Shandon Renmin, 1992.

WangGuowei 王國維, *Gu Shi Xin Zheng* 《古史新證》. Changsha: Hunan Renmin Press, 2010.

Wang Guowei 王國維. *Guan tang ji lin* 《觀堂集林》. 2nd. rev. ed. Beijing: Zhonghua, 1959.

Wang Hongbin 王宏斌, *Emperor's Art ‧ Han Fei Zi and Chinese Culture*《中國帝王術‧〈韓非子〉與中國文化》. Kaifeng: Henan University Press, 1995.

WangHuanlin 王煥林,*The Correction of Exegesis of the Qin Bamboo Slips of Liye*《里耶秦簡校詁》. Beijing: China Federation of Literary and Art Circles Press, 2007.

Wang Huaping 王化平, The Search of the Way of Being an Official in Qin Dynasty Unearthed at Yumeng and the Related Questions 《秦簡〈為吏之道〉及相關問題研究》[D], Chengdu, Sichuan University, 05/2003.

Wang Hui 王輝, Chen Shaorong 陳紹榮, and Wang Wei 王偉. *A General Survey of Qin Characters*《秦文字通論》. Beijing: CHUNG WHA Book Company, 2016.

Wang Hui 王輝, Try to analyze: Servants are adjudicated, for servants' the household is not adjudicated 試析"坐隸，隸不坐戶". *Journal of MudanJiang Normal University* 《牡丹江師範學院學報（哲學社會科學版）》, 2010: 59-62.

Wang Liqi 王利器. *Shi ji zhu yi 4 vols.*《史記注譯》. Xi'an: San Qin, 1988.

Wang Ning 王寧, Reading Han Scripts of Peking University of *Cang* 北大漢簡《蒼頡篇》讀劄（上）, The research center of the newly excavated document of Fudan 復旦大學出土文獻與古文字研究中心, 22/02/2016, http://www.gwz.fudan.edu.cn/Web/Show/2744

Wang Quan ed. 王權主編, *History of Chinese primary school mathematics teaching* 《中國小學數學教學史》. Jinan: Shandong Education Publishing House, 1996.

Wang Shaodong 王紹東. *Cultural factors behind Qin's rise and fall*《秦朝興亡的文化探討》. Huhehaote: Neimenggu Daxue Press.2004.

Wang Xianqian 王先謙. *Han shu bu zhu* 《漢書補註》. Changsha, 1900; rpt. In reduced facsimile, Taipei: Yiwen, 1955.

Wang Xueli. *The History of Qin Dynasty Material Culture*. Xi'an: San Qin Publishing House, 1994.

Wang Yanan 王亞南. 1981. *Zhongguo guanliao zhengzhi yanjiu* 中國官僚政治研究 *[A study of China's bureaucratic politic]*. Beijing: Zhongguo Shehui Kexue Press.

Wang Yanhui 王彥輝,*The Research of Han society and the Two Year Laws of Zhangjiashan* 《張家山漢簡〈二年律令〉與漢代社會研究》. Beijing: Zhonghua Book Company, 2010.

Wang Yusheng 王渝生, *History of Chinese Mathematics*《中國算學史》. Shanghai: Shanghai Renmin Press, 2006.

Wang Zijin 王子今, *Child Life of Han Dynasty*《漢代兒童生活》. Xi'an: San Qin Chu Ban She 三秦出版社, 2012.

Watson, Burton, trans. *Records of the Grand Historian. 3 vols.* New York: Columbia University Press, 1961, 1963.

Watson, Burton, trans. *The Complete Works of Chuang Tzu*. New York: Columbia University Press, 1968.

Watson, William. *China Before the Han Dynasty*. New York: Praeger, 1961.

Wilkinson Endymion. *Chinese History a New Munual 4 Edition*. Cambridge: Harvard University Asia Center for the Harvard-Yenching Institute, 1998; rpt. 2015.

WU Shuchen 武樹臣, Probe into the Cause of Changing 'Fa' into 'Lu' in the Kingdom of Qin 秦改法為律原因考. *The Jurist*《法學家》, 2011: 28-40.

Wu, Lina 武麗娜, and Wang Shujin 王樹金. 2005. Zongfa thought in Qin-Han law 試論秦漢法律中的宗法思想. *Qin wenhua luncong*2012: 507-17.

Xia Hanyi 夏含夷. Xi Zhou zhi shuaiwei 西周之衰微.*Wen gu zhi xin lu*《溫故知新錄》. Taipei: Daohe, 1997.

Xia Nai 夏鼐. *Kaoguxue he kejishi*《考古學和科技史》. Beijing: Kexue, 1979.

Xiao, Gongchuan (蕭公權)and F. W Mote. *A History of Chinese Political Thought*. Princeton: Princeton Legacy Library, 1979.

Xu Fuguan 徐復觀. *Zhongguo renxing lun shi* 《中國人性論史》. Taizhong: Donghai Daxue, 1963.

Xu Weimin 徐衛民, and He ruikun 賀潤坤. *Brief Introduction of the political thoughts of Qin*《秦政治思想述略》. Xi'an: Shangxi People's Education Press, 1995.

Xu, Fuguan 徐復觀.*History of thought in the Eastern and Western Han* 《兩漢思想史》. Taibei: Taiwan Xuesheng Press. 1979.

Xu, Zhuoyun and Katheryn M. Linduff. *Western Chou Civilization*. New Haven: Yale University Press, 1988.

Yan Gengwang 嚴耕望. *Chung-kuo ti-fang hsing-cheng chih-tu shih: Ch'in Han ti-fang hsing-cheng chih-tu2 vols.*《中國地方行政制度史:秦漢地方行政制度》. Taipei: Institute of History and Philology, 1964.

Yan Gengwang 嚴耕望. Selection of Yan Gengwang's historical writings 《嚴耕望史學論文選集》. Taibei: Lianjing Chuban Gongsi.1991.

Yan, Buke 閻步克. Musicians and scribes: essays on traditional political culture and institutions 《樂師與史官：傳統政治文化與政治制度論集》. Beijing: Sanlian Shudian.2001.

Yang Bojun, trans. *Mengzi*《孟子譯著》. Beijing: Zhonghua Press.1980.

Yang Kuan 楊寬. *Ch'in Shih-huang*《秦始皇》. Shanghai: Jen-min Ch'u-pan-she, 1956.

Yang Kuan 楊寬. *Gushi xintan*《古史新探》. Beijing: Zhonghua, 1965.

Yang Kuan 楊寬. *Shang Yang pien-fa*《商鞅變法》. Shanghai: Jen-min Ch'u-pan-she, 1955.

Yang Kuan 楊寬. Shi Qingchuan Qin du de tianmu zhidu 釋青川秦牘的田畝制度. *Wenwu* 1982(7): 83-5.

Yang Kuan 楊寬. *Zhanguo shi*《戰國史》. Shanghai: Shanghai Renmin,1980.

Yang Xiangkui 楊向奎. *Zhongguo gudai shehui yu gudai sixiang yanjiu*《中國古代社會與古代思想研究》. Shanghai: RenminPress, 1964.

Yang, Lien-sheng. *Studies in Chinese institutional history*. Cambridge, Mass.: harvard Univ. Press, 1961.

Yang, Shiqun 楊師群. *Dong Zhou Qin Han shehui zhuanxing yanjiu/ A study on social transformations during the Eastern Zhou, Qin, and Han*《東周秦漢社會轉型研究》. Shanghai: Shanghai Guji Press. 2003.

Yang, Xiangkui 楊向奎. *Zong Zhou shehui yu liyue wenming/Western Zhou society and its civilization of rites and music*《宗周社會與禮樂文明》. Beijing: Renming Press.1992.

Yang, Xiong and Jeffrey S Bullock. Yang Xiong, *Philosophy of the Fa Yan*. Highlands, N.C.: Mountain Mind Press, 2011.

Yates, Robin. "New Light on Ancient Chinese Military Texts: Notes on Their Nature and Evolution, and the Development of Military Specialization in Warring States China." TP 1988 (74): 211-48.

Ye Xiaoyan 葉小燕. Qin mu chutan 秦墓初探. *Kaogu*《考古》. 1982.1: 65-73.

Yu Haoliang 于豪亮. Shi Qingchuan Qin mu mudu 釋青川秦墓木牘. *Wenwu* 1982.1: 22-4.

Yu Weizhao 余偉釗. *Xian Qin Liang han kaoguxue lunji*《先秦兩漢考古學論集》. Beijing: Wenwu, 1985.

Yu Xingwu 于省吾. "Lüelun Xi Zhou jinwen zhong de liu shi he ba shi ji qi tuntian zhi" 略倫西周金文中的六師和八師及屯田制. *Kaogu* 《考古》. 1964(3): 152-5.

Yu Zongfa 余宗發, *The study of thoughts and systems of Qin Bamboo Slip of Yunmeng* 《雲夢秦簡中思想與制度鈞摭》. Taipei: Wenjin Press, 1992.

Yu, Haoliang 于豪亮, and Li Junming 李均明. Qinjian suo fanying de junshi zhidu/Military institutions as reflected in Qin bamboo slips 秦簡所反映的軍事制度. *Yunmeng qinjian yanjiu.* Beijing: Zhongghua Press.1981.

Yuan Ke 袁珂. *Shan hai jing jiaozhu*《山海經校注》. Shanghai: Guji, 1980.

Yuan Ke 袁珂. *Zhongguo gudai shenhua*《中國古代神話》. Rev. ed., Beijing: Zhonghua, 1960.

Yün-meng Ch'in-mu chu-chien cheng-li Hsiao-tsu 雲夢秦墓竹簡整理小組. Yün-meng Ch'in chien shih-wen 雲夢秦簡釋文. 3parts. *Wenwu,* 1976(6): 11-14; 1976(7): 1-10; 1976(8): 17-37.

Yün-meng Shui-hu-ti Ch'in mu pien-hsieh tsu 雲夢睡虎地秦墓編寫組. *Yünmeng Shui-hu-ti Ch'in mu*《雲夢睡虎地秦墓》. Beujing: Wen-wu Ch'u-pan-she, 1981.

Zhai, Jiangyue 翟江月. *The Spring and Autumn of Lü Buwei, vol. I -III (Chinese-English).* 《呂氏春秋》Ⅰ-Ⅲ；漢英對照. Guilin: Guangxi Normal University Press, 2005.

Zhang Jinguang 張金光. Shilun Qin zi Shang Yang bianfa hou de tude zhidu/On Qin's land ownership system after Shang Yang's reforms 試論秦自商鞅變法後的土地制度. *Zhongguoshi Yanjiu* 1983(2): 26-41.

Zhang Jinguang 張金光, *The Research of Qin's System*《秦制研究》. Shanghai: Shanghai Guji Press, 2004.

Zhang Longhua 張隆華, and Zeng Zhongshan 曾仲珊. *History of Education of Language and Literature of ancient China*《中國古代語文教育史》. Chengdu: Sichuan Education PressSichuan Education Press, 2003.

Zhang Shuangli, Zhang Wanbin, Yin Guoguang, and Chen Tao, annotated. *Master Lü's Spring and Autumn Annals*《呂氏春秋譯注》. Beijing: Zhonghua Press. 2007.

Zhang Xiaolei 張孝蕾, The Study of Sealed Postmortem Shi 睡虎地秦簡《封診式》研究 [D], Changsha, Hunan University, 05/2013.

Zhang, Jinfan 張晉藩. *Zhongguo fazhishi luncong/ assys on China's history of law* 中國法治史論叢. Beijing: Falü Press.1982.

Zhang, Zhengming 張正明. *The history of Chu*《楚史》. Wuhan: Hubei Jiaoyu Press. 1995.

Zhao Chao 趙超, An Investigation and Analysis of the Anonymous Pronoun "Yi"in "Feng Zhen Shi《封診式》中隱名代詞「乙」的考察分析. *Journal of Chongqing University of Arts and Sciences*《重慶文理學院學報》, 2017: 57-63.

Zhaojiuxiang 趙久湘, and Li Mingxiao 李明曉, *The Organization and Research of the Widely Scattered Qin Bamboo Slips during Warring States*《散見戰國秦漢簡帛法律文獻整理與研究》. Chongqing: Southwest China Normal University Press, 2011.

Zhao, Dingxin 趙鼎新. *The Confucian-Legalist State*. Oxford: Oxford University Press, 2015.

ZhengLiangshu 鄭良樹, *Acritical Biography if Shang Yang*《商鞅評傳》. Nanjing: Nanjing University Press, 2001.

ZhengLiangshu 鄭良樹, *Shang Yang and His School*《商鞅及其學派》. Shanghai: Shanghai Guji Press, 1989.

Zhou, Guixi 周桂細. *Qin Han sixiang shi/ History of Thought during Qin and Han*《秦漢思想史》. Shijiazhuang: Hebei Renmin Press. 2000.

ZhuHonglin 朱紅林, *The Explanation Collection on the Two Year Laws of Zhangjiashan Bamboo Slips*《張家山漢簡〈二年律令〉》集釋. Beijing: Social Sciences Academic Press, 2005.

Zhu Zhenghui 朱振輝, The Characteristic of Ruling of Official: from the Way to Be a Good Official of Qin Bamboo slips 從秦簡《為吏之道》看秦國的吏治特色. Journal of *Historical Science*《史學月刊》, 2011: 129-131.

Zhuang Chunbo 莊春波. *A Critical Biography of HAN WUDI*. Nanjing: Nanjing University Press, 2002.

Zou Dahai 鄒大海, *The Rising of Chinese Mathematics and the Mathematics of Pre-Qin*. Zhengzhou: Hebei science technology Press, 2011.

後記

　　這本書的緣起，來自一個小小的人生相遇。在本科畢業之際，我參加了澳門一個大型的國際學術會議，有幸認識了我的博士導師張偉保教授，此後，我們就結下了不解之緣。本書部分篇章曾以個人名義單獨發表，也有多篇是與張教授合作完成，並在不同的學術會議中發表。多年來多次獲得兩岸教育史研究專家的指正，如劉羨冰校長、劉海峰教授、周愚文教授、鄭潤培教授等的親切鼓勵，本人在此表示由衷的感謝。本書的最後修改曾得到鄭振偉教授的悉心指正，使本書的內容得以進一步提升。

　　從萌發要寫這本書的念頭，到清晰的明白完成這本書所需要克服的重重困難，關關難過關關過，最終這本書得以完成，總算是給這幾年苦心鑽研學術的自己一個交代。

　　一次次通宵達旦地翻閱新出土文獻，一輪輪惡補教育學的質性量化知識，一回回在教材史理論框架的角度下整理無盡的中英資料數據，沒有張偉保教授的幫助，我沒辦法堅持下來。

　　還好，這本書的纂寫最終小小的告一段落。

　　最感謝張偉保教授，沒有他的教導和支持，我不可能堅持下來。張偉保教授身教言傳地向他的學生們呈現了一位優秀的老師，一位學術涵養高超的學者，一個以仁義禮智信作為人生信條的人，應該是怎樣的。

　　感謝張文韜先生一路照顧情緒化的我，陪伴是最樸實最真摯的愛。

　　感謝我的父母讓我徜徉在知識的海洋裡並為我阻擋了許多生活繁瑣的叨擾。

　　感謝澳門大學的 rado，有了他們的大力支持，才有 the Teaching Material of the Legalist's School before Han Dynasty（編號：MYRG2014-00059-FED）

這個項目的完成。

　　最後要感謝澳門大學和澳門大學教育學院，它給了我一個開闊的平臺，並為我打開了一扇通向世界學術的門。

　　還有好多人在我這艱難的一路走來給予了我各種各樣的幫助，不能一一道謝但我都銘記於心。人生的道路總是孤獨的，但有些人卻能照亮並溫暖我前行的路。

溫如嘉

誌於澳門大學教育學院

二〇二〇年九月二十日

The New Asia Arts and Business Academic Series   1707001

Official as Teacher: An Investigation on the Newly Excavated Document of Legalist School in Qin China

Author   Wen Ru Jia、Cheung Wai Po
Administrative Editor   Lu Yu Shan
Proofreader   Zeng Guei Ci

Publisher   Lin Cing-Jhang
General Manager   Liang Jin-shing
Printed by   Sen Lan Printing Co., Ltd.
Distributed by   WAN JUAN LOU BOOKS CO., Ltd.6F.-3, No. 41, Sec. 2,
                 Roosevelt Rd.,Da'an Dist.,Taipei City 106, Taiwan
                 Tel (02)23216565   FAX (02)23218698
                 Email servicr@wanjuan.com.tw

ISBN   978-986-478-364-9
Price   NT$300

新亞文商學術叢刊   1707001

以吏為師：新出土法家教材新探

作　　者　溫如嘉、張偉保
責任編輯　呂玉姍
特約校稿　曾貴祺
發 行 人　林慶彰
總 經 理　梁錦興
印　　刷　博創印藝文化事業有限公司
發　　行　萬卷樓圖書股份有限公司
　　　　　臺北市羅斯福路二段 41 號 6 樓之 3
　　　　　電話 (02)23216565 傳真 (02)23218698
　　　　　電郵 SERVICE@WANJUAN.COM.TW
ISBN   978-986-478-364-9
2020 年 10 月初版
定　價　新臺幣 300 元